Whole Whog Catalog

Whole Whog Catalog

by
Victor Langer
Leslie Anderson
Bob Ross

illustrated by
Leslie Anderson

with a preface by
Chevy Chase

Times
BOOKS

Published by TIMES BOOKS, a division of
Quadrangle/The New York Times Book Co., Inc.
Three Park Avenue, New York, N.Y. 10016

Published simultaneously in Canada by
Fitzhenry & Whiteside, Ltd., Toronto.

Copyright © 1980 by Victor Langer, Leslie Anderson, Bob Ross

Library of Congress Cataloging in Publication Data:

Langer, Victor.
    Whole whog catalog.

    Includes index.
    1. Manufactures—Anecdotes, facetiae, satire, etc.
2. Catalogs, Commercial—Anecdotes, facetiae, satire, etc.
I. Anderson, Leslie, joint author. II. Ross, Bob, 1946-
joint author. III. Title. PN6231.M23L3 1980 602.9′4 80-5353
ISBN 0-8129-0953-4

Manufactured in the United States of America

Cover Illustration: Leslie Anderson

Book Design: the Authors

Type Composition: Sigmagraph

"You only wallow once
in the sty of life.
So go whole hog
and pig out while you can."
—Francis Bacon

Preface by Chevy Chase

I have personally known the authors of the *Whole Whog Catalog* for many a long month. Victor Langer and I went to college together. Okay? Perhaps best known for his brilliant translation of Rainer Maria Rilke's *Ten Elegies,* which have never been published, Mr. Langer is, perhaps, best known for this.

Leslie Anderson, most responsible for the accurate illustrations of the *W.W.C.* merchandise, and the gifted art designer and co-writer of this compilation, is, to my knowledge, not a man. If she is, he has a beautiful chest. We did not go to college together. But we will, if asked.

Bob "Ross" is, from what Vic and Les tell me, not really a major part of this book, though the original transcript was entirely written and illustrated by him, yet, tragically, irretrievably lost in a bedroom explosion in 1973. It was the only copy. Since that time Ross has all but abandoned the thought of updating, and has only occasionally "offered some thoughts."

When the authors first contacted me some six years ago, they asked that I might be a "guinea pig" of sorts, and sent me many of the items herein catalogued, plus some which are not to be found in the *W.W.C.* Personally, I found their request insulting and confusing. Money talks, however.

Since that time I have become actually quite attached to these items. I wear the *Whole Whog™ Leisure Wet Suit* to all Hollywood parties attended by the press or the Cousteaus. A *W.W.C. Toilet Seatbelt* can be found as a courtesy in my guest bathroom. A continual source of delight and fascination to myself and my neighbor is my *Batmobile™ Bat Feeder/Guano Accumulator.*

Among those products not listed in this all but comprehensive work, are a few for which I have a special feeling. Perhaps they were omitted purely because there were simply not enough in stock. Perhaps not. Neither explanation is worth pursuit. Let me tell you, the reader, I assume, about one or two of these unlisted sundries, will you?

My summer homes in the hills of Austria boast the protection and fine styling of the **W.W.C. Barking Doorknobs**™ (optional extras include touch-activated taped recordings of a filtered deep male voice confirming over the telephone that an approaching patrol car is within two kilometers, or unfiltered confident "007"-like challenges such as: "Come on in, Sissy. Ready to Die?", accompanied by realistic sound effects of loading and cocking a 12 gauge shotgun; knob-activated anxious rattlesnake sound effects— Dolby Sound). License unnecessary, speakers not included.

W.W.C. Pants Wetter™
Includes bulb and tube with shoulder harness for armpit control. Great for getting out of or into embarrassing situations.

W.W.C. Incredible Talking™ **Avocados**
A bit of craftsmanship, a novelty item, a conversation piece. Come in pairs.

W.W.C.Egg Scanner™
Find out in a jiffy if your eggs are hard-boiled, fertilized, or empty.

W.W.C. Lawn 'n' Garden Shampoo™
pH balanced; great for moss.

W.W.C. Mattress Tags™
Stay out of trouble and avoid embarrassing confrontations with overzealous Mattress Police.

W.W.C. Nose™ **Deodorant**
Stops odors from reaching the nose for hours.

W.W.C. Panty Hose™
Actually cleans your most delicate undergarments from the inside while you're on the go.

W.W.C. Step-On-Lift-Off Velcro™ **Sock Remover**
No bending over. No back problems. No threat of athlete's hand.

W.W.C. Split-End Braider™
Corn-row those unwanted split-ends for a delightful and confusing look.

W.W.C. Bird™ **Jacuzzi**
A must for bird-watchers and birds. They stay longer; relax while you do.

Well, there are many more. And most are included in this massive document, which, should you find it necessary to read after my preface, will stimulate you for weeks to come. Enjoy this coffee table masterpiece in good health, and give my best to your wife. I couldn't.

CHEVY CHASE
September, 1980
Austria

The World of Whole Whog™

Go Whole Whog™

The world of Whole Whog™ is *your* world. It's a world where you go all out, without inhibition, for all you're worth. Your number one interest is getting more out of life, and we're keeping up with you. In this world the look is lavish, the feeling is free, and the touch is yours. More and more, it's happening for you. More and more it's clear there's really no need to hold back. You just reach out for what you need. You help yourself. You go Whole Whog™.

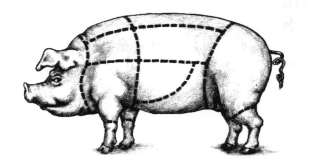

Service with a Snort™

Some big retailers don't give a snort about you after sale, but Whole Whog™ always stands behind you with parts and service . . . and most important of all, a pleasant snort.

Charging Wild Boar™
Charge Plan

Give yourself credit and make it easy on yourself. The Whole Whog™ charge card with the familiar Charging Wild Boar™ allows you to charge whenever you feel the urge. If you need to charge in person for self-serving shopping, your Whole Whog™ Outlet is ready when you are. Or if you prefer, just pick up the phone and say "Charge!" in the comfort of your own sty.

Guarantee
of Satiation

If at any time you are in any way not satiated, just give
a squeal and we will promptly indulge you with an
exchange, an adjustment, or a full refund. Above all,
we want to do everything we can to make sure that you
are completely satiated.

The Whole Whog
Squeal of Approval™

This is the Whole Whog Squeal of Approval™. It
appears throughout the *Whole Whog Catalog* to
indicate certain items we feel especially good about.
They cover the field from glamour to gadgetry,
carrying our pledge of high-on-the-hog quality.

Contents

The Feeding Frenzy

The Comfort Zone

The Body Shop

Contents continued

Apparel: Intimate and Otherwise

Objets d'Art

Social Security Systems

Protected by **Pinkerton's**

Contents continued

The Pet Kingdom

Yard 'n' Garden

Nonhuman Pest Control

Contents continued

Autosuggestion

Potpourri

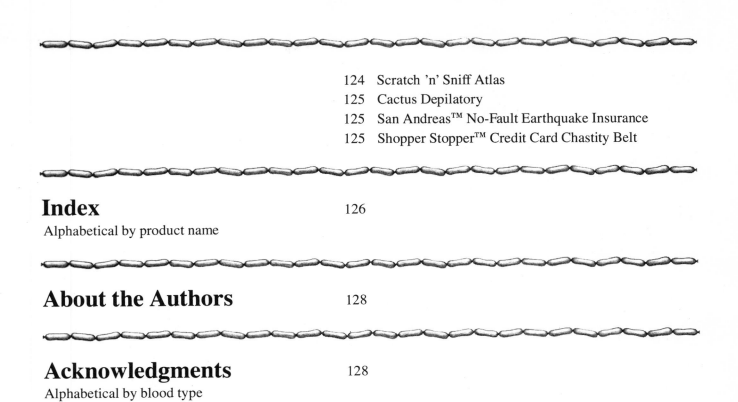

Index

Alphabetical by product name

About the Authors

Acknowledgments

Alphabetical by blood type

The
Feeding
Frenzy

Endangered Species Preserves

A veritable zoo on a shelf. This collection of ten magnificent endangered animals is preserved for posterity as commemorative gourmet spreads and confections. Each is vacuum-packed in its own laboratory bottle with glass stopper. Labels are fine reproductions of specially commissioned color etchings. Help yourself to:

Seedless Black Pelican Preserves
Red Wolf Jelly
Three-toed Sloth Jam
Orangutan Marmalade
Candied Sperm Whale
California Condor Compote
Whooping Crane Pâté
American Bald Eagle Aspic
Snail-darter Caviar
Pickled Puma

Keep and treasure for years to come, or serve and enjoy now. No preservatives—refrigerate after opening.
5% of profit goes to help prevent extinction.   39.95

The Kitchen Maniac™

The powerful and creative food processor that doesn't know when to stop. There's nothing it won't do. It goes to any length to please you. At your command the Maniac whips a meal into shape, creating vegetable mayhem, and beating eggs into submission. Makes short work of dressings, even batters. Renders chicken fat harmless, makes mincemeat out of sausages, and vice versa (with meatballer attachment). Leftovers? The Kitchen Maniac™ wreaks havoc on leftovers. Guaranteed ten years to life. Complete with "straight-jacket" cozy to restrain unit when not in use.
Warning: Follow normal industrial safety precautions. When unit is set on "Rampage", wear safety goggles and hair net, or stand in an adjoining room.
Manufacturer not responsible for human error.   329.95

Ham on the Range: A Ballad

Ham, ham on the range,
Where the links and the patties sauté.
What once was a herd is now cut by a third,
And the sties are not crowded all day.

The "Cooking with Brains" Cookbook

To be a smart cook today takes brains. Brains are versatile, economical, a goldmine of protein*, and easier to prepare than you might think—in fact, after thorough brainwashing, the meat is actually quite easy to deal with. This brilliant new cookbook by Julia Brainchild shows you exactly how to get the most out of your brains. *Cooking with Brains* contains 101 kitchen-tested recipe brainstorms. Prepare tempting brain sensations like Headcheeseburgers, Scatterbrain Stew, Refried Prefrontal Lobes, Headlong Sausage with Scrambled Brains, "Uranium Cranium" Nuclear Headcheese Nuggets, "Heads-Up" Brainpan Loaf with Gray Matter Sauce, Head-over-heels Tossed Salad, Egghead Omelet with Cerebral Parsley Garnish, and a heady extravaganza called "The Force"—a whole brain encased in a shimmering, wobbling, dome-shaped clear aspic. The book is also filled with lots of brainy tips and ideas, for example: don't pick your brain—a brief brainwashing will suffice; and don't beat your brain—tenderize it by long, slow cooking. So the next time you're wondering what to serve your hungry headhunter, use your brains and dish out something he can really sink his teeth into. Think about it.   9.95

*For free nutritional information write to The Brain Board, P.O. Box 10, Porc Loines, Iowa 60211.

Psychic Deli Mobile

A delicious work of art with magic powers. Real delicatessen meats fashioned into a handsome mobile that's not only decorative and edible, but useful as a psychic tool. Help induce hypnosis by staring at the slowly swaying and turning forms. Practice psycho-kinesis—try to move the meat with your mind (suspend away from heaters, air-conditioners, and open windows) or use it like a Ouija Board to answer the questions "Who...", "Where..." or "What...". Ask the question telepathically, and all the salamis which are horizontally hung will converge to "point" at the person or object (correct answer must be within the room). Artful design graces any area: hang it as the aromatic centerpiece of a room, accent a foyer or landing, or lend savory charm to an uninteresting corner. 7 lbs.:   32.95

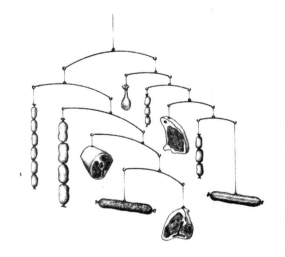

Heads of State™
U.S. Presidents Patty Press

Patty prestige! Now you can press your patties into the profile of a president, and create festive oval office burgers. This patriotic patty press has interchangeable molds for all 36 U.S. heads of state—throw a party without repeating a president, and always have everyone's favorite president's head on hand. High-pressure frame and deep-relief molds help form features that stay sharp even after cooking. Be creative with garnishes—try parsley sideburns for Lincoln, a scallion-bunch pony-tail for Jefferson, or a gala cherry tomato nose for Ulysses S. Grant. How about a lacy ascot of butter lettuce for Washington? Use an onion ring monocle for Teddy Roosevelt, or try a Nixonburger with a leek instead of an onion! Molds have Face Saver™ nonstick surfaces to release meat completely for smooth, firm cheeks without pocks or ripples (except for Lincoln). Excess meat which squeezes out around edge of face is automatically shaved away by patented press-frame for a clean profile the first time, every time. Entire head shrinks slightly with cooking, but features remain proportionally correct. Two patty sizes for liberal or conservative appetites; size dependent upon president's party: Republican patties are ¼ pound, all other parties' patties are ½ pound. (All parties' patties have same face area for uniformity, but Republicans are shallower.) Plan your own two-party patty party. 29.95

Lincoln

Developing Nations Cookie Cutter Set

The fun and delicious way to keep abreast of foreign economics in a rapidly changing world. Make tempting, topical, and topographical cookies in the shape of 12 developing nations, including Chad, Zambia, Oman, Sri Lanka, and Togo. Decorate with raisins for principal cities, chocolate chips for mountain ranges, cooked vermicelli for main rivers, and jimmies for forests. (Includes maps for key features reference.) You'll receive a free annual supplement to inform you of cookie cutters that have become available for new developing nations and of those nations that have moved off the list. 4.79

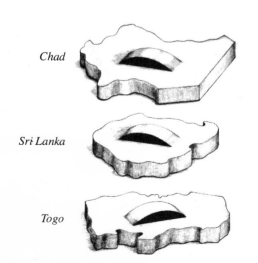

Chad

Sri Lanka

Togo

Kelp Helper™

Kelp, aptly named "The Chicory of the Sea", is a valuable high-protein staple crop that until recently was just floating around. Now kelp has come to stay, but don't let familiarity breed contempt—helping after helping of plain kelp just won't do. So help that kelp—perk it up ten great ways with Kelp Helper™. There's Kelp Quiche, Kelp Creole, Devilled Kelp Loaf, Kelp-Ka-Bob, Kelp Cous-cous, Carrot Kelpcakes, Kelp Wellington, Kelp en Croute, Kelp Crêpes, Kippered Kelp Casserole.   All only 1.19

Agent Orange Ade™

Agent Orange Ade™—the first ade of the future. Formerly an effective defoliant, Agent Orange returns as a sparkling beverage to perk up your sagging taste; it picks up where it leaves off. Agent Orange Ade™ is a power-packed potion pumped up with massive doses of high-potency sustained-release synthetic megavitamins. Just one glass of A.O.A. has a vitamin content equal to 20 gallons of the leading natural orange ade. Real pulp is added for the look and feel of fresh-squeezed. Has been drunk in orbit; it's A-ok with A.O.A. Liter: 1.29

Alka-Cola™

Here's one medicine you won't mind taking a dose of: a combination pain reliever and refreshing soft drink. Alka-Cola™ has an antacid to settle your stomach, carbonation to help free trapped gas, buffered aspirin to go to work on your headache, caffeine to give you a lift, and great thirst-quenching cola taste to give you a smile. Convenient effervescent tablets turn tap water into a full bodied dark-amber cola in seconds. Serve on the rocks, or mix with rum to make cocktails that have the morning-after cure built right in. No more heavy liquids to lug home from the store, no bottles to return, and no cans to recycle. 36 Tablet pack (makes ten gallons):   1.89

Every hog has his day.

International Blenders

This line of worldly multi-speed blenders now makes it possible for a variety of cultures to blend without getting mixed up. Just a turn of a dial lets the user view the speed names in his native language—no more tedious translation of a large number of hardly distinguishable verbs, and no more guesswork. Speed ranges are designed with *your* culture in mind. (Closest English equivalents of speed names are given below.)

First World Blender

A twelve speed, four language blender. Speed names appear in either English, French, German, or Japanese. The base is brushed chrome; the jar is of high-impact plastic. Speeds are: *churn—glut—sate—cloy—sully—spurn—swagger—bloat—distend—burgeon—flaunt—vaunt.* With instant impulse button.   89.95

Second World Blender

A ten speed, two language blender. Speed names in Russian and Chinese. Base in khaki wool serge; copper "artillery shell" jar with bamboo handle. Speeds are: *beat—whip—purge—liquidate—extol—rescind—exacerbate—brandish—expunge—relent.*   14.95

Third World Blender

The revolutionary six speed, three language blender. Speed names in Spanish, Hindustani, Swahili. Base in real grass mat, with "gourd" jar. Speeds are: *seethe—wince—vex—skulk—teem—foment.*   9.95

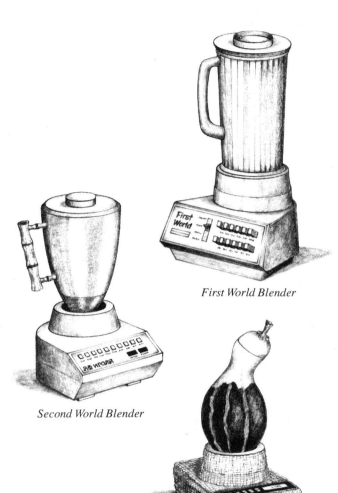

First World Blender

Second World Blender

Third World Blender

A Whole Whog™ Pork Tip

First-Aid for a toothache: place a small frozen pork breakfast link between the lip and gum until you can get attention. Change every half hour.

Abstinence makes the hog grow harder.

Chew 'n' Tell™ Edible Telephone

A functioning phone that doubles as a delicious high-protein snack. The entire unit is edible: shell, chassis, internal components, coil cord, everything! You can eat your way right down to the wall jack. Next time you get the munchies on a long call, just help yourself without having to put your party on hold to run to the kitchen. You can nibble away the entire shell, and unit will still function properly. As long as you don't bite an internal component you won't get cut off. Hearty appetite? Just hang it up, unplug at wall jack, and really dig in to finish off your set. If you forget to unplug and bite into a live unit, don't worry— normal telephone voltage is not high enough to do much more than make your gums tingle. Have your own calling party: place a conference call to friends who have edible units, and enjoy a chat over refreshments without leaving your phone. FCC, FDA, and UL approved. Perfect for fallout shelters—you're covered whether the emergency is communication or nutrition. Four great flavors: Spumoni, Halvah, Pork Party-Loin, and the new low-calorie Watercress Diet Phone. All flavors available in Trimline*, Princess*, Standard Desk, or Standard Wall; and in Touch-Tone* or rotary Dial.

Spumoni Trimline Touch Tone:	26.79
Halvah Trimline Touch-Tone:	24.89
Pork Party-Loin Trimline Touch-Tone:	27.79
Watercress Trimline Touch-Tone Diet-Phone:	23.49
Spumoni Princess Touch-Tone:	29.99
Halvah Princess Touch-Tone:	25.69
Pork Party-Loin Princess Touch-Tone:	26.69
Watercress Princess Touch-Tone Diet-Phone:	25.79
Spumoni Desk Touch-Tone:	24.59
Halvah Desk Touch-Tone:	23.49
Pork Party-Loin Desk Touch-Tone:	21.99
Watercress Desk Touch-Tone:	22.99
Spumoni Wall Touch-Tone:	23.49
Halvah Wall Touch-Tone:	27.99
Pork Party-Loin Wall Touch-Tone:	26.79
Watercress Wall Touch-Tone Diet-Phone	29.89

For rotary Dial subtract 1.89   *Trademark of AT&T Co.

A Whole Whog™ Ham Hint

Save water by putting a canned ham in your toilet tank. Depending on the size of your ham, you'll save up to two gallons per flush. And your ham will keep cool until you're ready to open and serve.

Breakfast Cereals

A nutritious assortment of breakfast entrees and anytime snacks in exciting new shapes and flavors.

Baconeers™

Festive pirate motif. Skull and crossbones shaped. Bacon flavor. High in nitrates, essential fats, and heavy metals.   89¢

Swinettes™

Pork butt shape and flavor. Tangy and colorful. Faithful miniatures. Great as hors d'oeuvres.   89¢

Mini Machos™

Puny puffed-up golden-brown buds of corn that pack a whallop. Chili flavor. Festive fist shape. For breakfast or fiesta.   79¢

Whole Whog's Corn Holes™

Spoon size rings of corn that stand up to milk. Great with fruit. Open wide.   1.19

Ham Checks™

Ham flavor and shape. Extra loud crackling takes over the breakfast table and perks up groggy eaters.   69¢

Frosted Corns 'n' Bunions™

Crunchy, lightly sweetened foot ailments.   59¢

Liver Spots™

Crude-fiber liver-flavored pellets in random sizes. Fast softening—add milk, swill. Handle the impassable naturally and start the day with a bang. Pass it on. 1.09

Rice Jerky™

The popular flavor of rice meets the fun shape of jerky for a great tasting tug of war.   98¢

A Whole Whog™ Ham Hint

Moving heavy furniture can be a drag. Put a thick slice of fatback under each leg for smooth sailing.

The Lard Gun™

Armed with The Lard Gun™ you're ready to open up new frontiers of food decoration. Don't limit yourself to sugary decorations on cakes and pastries—now you can embellish the main dish itself, and lard is the perfect medium. Cover your next roast, ham, or meat loaf with rosettes and ribbons of lard, write a message in florid script, or create a scene. The Lard Gun™ makes it easy to hit the spot with festive decorations. Variable trigger gives you fingertip control to put the lard right where you want it. New no-mess lard cartridges are a snap to change. Just load up, take aim, and fire away. The versatile Lard Gun™ also makes short work of caulking and sealing jobs around sinks, tubs, windows, and baseboards. It even fills holes in plaster walls: shoot a little dollop of lard on the trouble spot, and smooth off with a butter knife. Gun includes three lard cartridges and book, *Discovering Animal Fat*.

The Lard Gun™ set:	12.95
Replacement Lard Cartridge:	.98

Fruit Probe

Take the guesswork out of ripeness testing. This sensitive device performs the many types of tests needed for different types of produce. It squeezes tomatoes, pinches grapes, presses pears, pokes peppers, palpates peaches, and more. There's even sonar capability for fruits that defy mechanical probing, such as kiwis and coconuts. Three probe tips cover the entire range of tests: tongs, pincers, and mini-ram. Just snap in the appropriate tip, set dial for fruit type, and Probe does the rest.　69.95

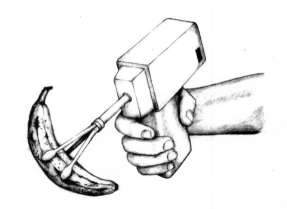

The Green Machine™ Lettuce Spray

Greens are great, but are they really worth the trouble? Tedious washing, spin-drying or time-consuming air drying, and storage problems are enough to give you the greens blues. Enter: the ever-green; a superfine spray of real lettuce that's always ready to go, in salads, on sandwiches, as a garnish, anywhere you need greens. Toss your keeper and spinner, and banish those wilted, soggy, and moldy heads that are always cluttering up the crisper. Great for camping too (not above 5,000 feet). New no-clog nozzle. Let us spray.

12 head can:　1.89

The Chicken Legger/Boner/Beaker™

At last a power boner that's man enough to handle the job. The Chicken Legger/Boner/Beaker™ is a five horsepower poultry processor that bones your bird by centrifugal force. Bone a large pullet in a minute, cleanly and completely, in a hands-off operation. Even a whopper. Just drop in hopper and watch for the "boned" light to come on. Then pullet out. With big bone bin for binges. Not just a great boner, but legs and beaks with the best of them. If you've really got a bone to pick and you've decided to move up to a high power boner, pick the Chicken Legger/Boner/Beaker™—and make no bones about it.   149.95

Tub o'Lard™ Deep Fat Fryer

The Tub o'Lard™ takes the cake for size, easily outweighing the competition. Deeper *and* fatter than other fryers, its huge capacity makes big big batches— colossal servings for the large, fat family. Wide body design can dish it out *and* take it—there's even ample room for a large-boned chicken. Rotund profile and stout rubber feet prevent spills. Extra heavy basket and super-size slotted spoon for jumbo loads.   88.88

Cordless George Washington Carver

You asked for it! We bring back by popular demand the patriotic and practical electric carving knife with the George Washington handle that was first offered by Whole Whog™ during the Bicentennial. The most famous of our founding fathers makes short work of big holiday birds, effortlessly cutting through resistance. When George runs down he slips into his recharging scabbard and in no time he's ready for more. One side of handsome handle has scene of Washington as a boy chopping down the cherry tree, the other side shows him as President cutting through red tape on the floor of the House. Scabbard depicts the embattled General wintering at Valley Forge.   59.95

Meat Beaters™ Meat Substitutes

If you can beat the meat habit you've got inflation licked. Nutritious Meat Beaters™ let you balance your budget as well as your diet by beating both high cost and cholesterol. And you placate predatory guilt without sacrificing animals at the table. Meat Beaters™ are not a blend—there's absolutely no meat content; they are a unique food creation of 100% vegetable protein with emulsifiers, flavoring agents, colorants, and high-stability preservatives. They represent the state-of-the-art of simulated foods: a Nobel Prize winning chemist* formulated the flavorings, and a noted cosmetic surgeon* developed the coloration, texture, and structure—accurate even down to bones, fat, and tendons. Guests will never guess it's not the real thing. Only your grocer will know for sure. And you don't have to stick to links and patties—you've got a wide USDA choice, even chops and roasts. No refrigeration needed. Two year shelf life. Mail order OK.

12 savory Breakfast Links (8 oz.):	.39
1 lb. assorted round and square "Lunchmeat" Slices:	.49
Four ¼ lb. juicy "Burger" Patties:	.59
Two center-cut "Pork" Chops:	.98
Large 4 lb. boneless "Beef" Rump Roast:	1.19

*Names on request.

Watermelon Seed Vacuum

Seedy melon? Don't let seeds spoil the fun of eating watermelon. This versatile lightweight fruit vacuum can seed half a large watermelon in less than 30 seconds. Patented vacuum prongs do the job without harming the flesh; there's no beater-bar to mangle your melon. Powerful suction for deep cleaning—right down to the rind. Large three-melon capacity and easy-empty seed cup—no more seed bags to buy! With headlight, and nozzles for cantaloupes, cucumbers, and grapes. Power baller attachment makes fruit salad easy.   69.95

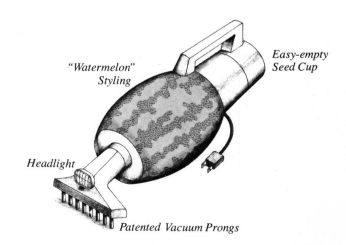

"Watermelon" Styling

Easy-empty Seed Cup

Headlight

Patented Vacuum Prongs

Hog's Law of Gastronomical Capacity

Infinite gastronomical capacity universally gravitates toward magnetic fields of corn.

Sheep Dip Party Dip

This dip is a real crowd-pleaser. Watch them all flock around: big dippers, little dippers, even the black sheep. Serve all three zesty flavors: Leg of Mutton, Rack of Lamb, and Mountain Oyster. Perfect viscosity makes for big chip appeal: dip has good cling, yet chips plow through easily without breaking or getting stuck. Graze on Sheep Dip and chips when you have the herd over for drinks. Here's to ewe.

Individual Dip:	.89
3 Assorted Dips:	1.98

The Meat Meter™

Meter the heat of your meat with this LED meat probe. It gives a constant display of temperature, and a read-out of meat done-ness on command: raw, medium-rare, medium, medium-well, or well-done. Leave it in to monitor meat throughout cooking—it can take the heat. Has the Meat Minder™ alarm, which sounds off when meat reaches a preset temperature. Big display is easy to see, even through the smoke of outdoor barbecues. Telescoping probe can handle chops and patties, and extends to penetrate deep into hams. Economical six pack lets you monitor the whole family's burgers at once. Dishwasher safe. Brushed chrome. Fahrenheit only.

Single Meat Meter™:	2.98
Meat Meter™ Six Pack:	10.95

Jerky Sampler

A savory assortment of Pork Jerky, Lamb Jerky, Jackal Jerky, Turkey Jerky, Gerbil Jerky, and traditional Beef Jerky, all packed in an attractive "stockyard" box with strips of jerky nestling in straw and surrounded by a mini rustic fence. It's time you discovered the joy of jerky, the satisfying and long-lasting treat. Whatever the occasion, jerky makes it. Jerky is a natural—don't try to resist it—enjoy jerky often. Take a jerky break for a quick pick-me-up. Try jerky with cocktails, jerky with friends, jerky alone, jerky any time of day. The Jerky Sampler is great as a gift, but hands off the temptation until you're ready to present.   19.97

The
Comfort
Zone

The Guilt Quilt

Indulge yourself in the ultimate cover-up. The Guilt Quilt is a motley patchwork of anxiety and apprehension pieced together with poignant portraits of the giants of guilt from science, literature, philosophy, and religion. Featured are Freud, Kafka, Kierkegaard, Luther, and many more. Bordered by intricate evil-eye fretwork and all handcrafted by Jewish matrons using a variation on the ancient forbidden stitch. Choose from Spread or Discomforter style. Further enhance your suffering with matching guilt-edged hair pillow shams. Now you have no excuse not to wrap yourself in premonitions, luxuriate in vague fear, and surround yourself with self-recrimination and gloom.

Spread or Discomforter.
Twin only: 439.95
(Full, Queen, and King not available.)

Guilt-edged Hair Pillow Shams: 49.95

Coffee Table Book Cover Club

Why go to the expense of coffee table books that are virtually never opened? Now get only the covers of those same impressive editions you've had your eye on, at a fraction of the cost. When you become a member we'll mail you five dummy books plus five covers; then every eight weeks you'll receive five new glossy covers from handsome works on art, photography, nature, travel, and sports. To be safe, some will be traditional subjects; others will cover more exotic themes to display your distinctive and varied tastes. You pay only 2.95 for each of 12 shipments. And take advantage of this introductory offer for new members: join now and receive for only 99¢ five dummy books and your first five covers:

Hang Gliders for Pets
Skiing on Rice
Big Ben from the Air
Skateboarding Micronesia
Cellulite Art

Cold hams, warm hog.

Pig in a Blanket™ Comforter

Pamper yourself with a soft and sensual security
blanket and wallow in this comforting sty design.
A background of luxuriant trampled straw is dappled
with dark glossy little patches of mud peeping through,
accented by glinting puddles of water, and casually
strewn with half-eaten corn cobs and an occasional
stool. Satiny acetate is plumply overstuffed with
polyester fiberfill.

Twin:	79.95
Full or Sow:	99.95
Boar:	109.95

Diesel Lounger

Get the look and feel of the big rig and put the hammer
down at home. Idle all day in this plush, full-feature
cab, just like a real cross-country 18-wheeler. Lounge,
recline, swivel, rock, and enjoy the 13″ in-dash color
TV, stereo headrest, CB radio, and three-way pulsating
heat massage for shoulders, lower back, and seat. All
functions are powered by an energy-efficient diesel
engine with 18 feet of flexible hose to vent your exhaust
out a window or up your chimney. Under-seat mini-frig
stocked with light beer. Snack console, shoulder
harness, pedal set, hi-low shifter, swing-away steering
column, and our Pile-Driver™ donut seat-cushion for
marathon lounging without discomfort. Watch for
Smokey over your Donkey in the twin oversized
side-view mirrors. Deep diamond-tufted upholstery
is leather/vinyl blend for the look and smell of real
leather with the convenience and economy of vinyl.
Request free color brochure.   39,999.95

Ham's Law

When adjacent hams are divided by the square
rootabegga raised to the power of multiple
hogarhythms, the sum of swine and coswine is well
proportional to pork pie arse squared.

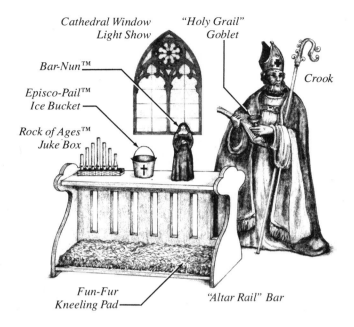

Cathedral Window Light Show

"Holy Grail" Goblet

Bar-Nun™

Crook

Episco-Pail™ Ice Bucket

Rock of Ages™ Juke Box

Fun-Fur Kneeling Pad

"Altar Rail" Bar

Heavenly No-Host Bar

After a day of hell, unwind and transcend it all with this unusual home bar ensemble which is an ecclesiastical extravaganza. Rest on fun-fur kneeling pads in front of a low "altar rail" bar and have your drinks served in a "holy grail" goblet by a bartender in real bishop's robes and mitre while you enjoy the stained glass "cathedral window" light show, with its pulsating rays straight out of Michelangelo. Accent the scene with fun and functional accessories like the "Quaker" shaker, the Episco-Pail™ ice bucket, "shepherd's staff" swizzle sticks, "Holy Roller" coasters, "swaddling clothes" drink cozies, a "serpent of Eden" corkscrew, "crown of thorns" party hats, or the amazing talking Bar-Nun™, which is really a miniature breath analyzer—just exhale on the vent in her habit and she'll tell you when to stop by discreetly whispering "Don't be a martyr." Choose from a staggering assortment of drinks and premixed cocktails: have a Bloody Mary, a Saint Thomas of Quinine, or a Christian Brothers with a holy water back; or for something more exotic try a Tabernacle Daiquiri, a Mormon Nailer, A San Franciscan Friar, a Solomon's Temple, an Easter Sunrise, a Last Stupor, an Immaculate Concoction, a Vodka Stigmata, or a Rusty Nail. For novices, there's the nonalcoholic Saint Francis the Sissy and Juice for Jesus. There are plenty of bar-top snacks, so if the spirit moves you, reach for a handful of cheese flavored Circumsnaps™, high fiber Holy Wheats™, double cross shaped Crucifixion Thins™, or zesty Jesus Crisps™ congregation-tested communion wafers. Use our recipes to make your own festive treats, like Baptismal Fondue, Blood Sausage Hors d'Oeuvres, or Pontius Pilaf. For musical inspiration you've got the Rock of Ages™ bar-mounted compact juke box with 36 favorite secular selections including *Sins You Went Away* by The Temptations, *Halo Goodbye* by the Satan Dolls, *Behind Her Pew* by Peter, Paul and Mary, *The Lone Manger* by Joltin' Joe and the Magi, *He Laid Me on the Altar of the Lord* by the Singing Nun, and *It Ain't the Meat it's the Methodist* by the Original Sins. For those who get too much into the spirit, there's our Born Again™ morning-after tablets to ease the pain of penance. And don't let your guests take it all for granted. After all, there's no host. Once they've been served, just pass the collection plate for tax-deductible contributions. They'll be talking in tongues.

Bar, kneeling pad, bishop's outfit, light show, 12 goblets, accessory set, 48 assorted premixed cocktails, snack sampler and recipes, juke box, 36 morning-after tablets: 498.95

Whole Whog™ Fireplace Set

Here's everything you need to get fired up in style and comfort: hogshead andirons, Pigpen™ fire screen, swine flue handle, pig sticker poker, pig iron tongs, boar's bristle broom, and Pigsty™ hovel shovel for ash cleanup. Bright brass plated or matte black enamel: 59.95

Laz-E-Jaw™ Recliner

Settle back in the awesome gaping jaws of a great white shark. You're in the first and only recliner to employ the principle of the waterbed. Tongue (seat) and palate (backrest) are fluid-filled so you float in stressless comfort. Never fear. Jawmatic™ power-recline gives you independent control of both upper and lower jaws at the touch of a tooth: last lower left incisor raises and lowers lower jaw; ninth upper right incisor tilts upper jaw forward and back. Select the position you like best, or for privacy, pull in your legs, close it up all the way, and be swallowed in seclusion. Reading light, stereo speakers, and oxygen supply are built right into roof of mouth. Sharkskin-look vinyl hide; padded white satin teeth; red velour tongue, palate, and uvula. With giant sea turtle ottoman. 495.95

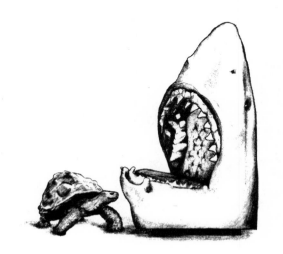

Video Hearth

This hot item is the state of the art in home fireplace convenience. High-realism video fire does away once and for all with fussing and fuming, dangerous flames, unpleasant smoke and odors, excessive heat, airborn soot, ash residue, and costly firewood and kindling. Includes videotape library of eight real hardwood fires, from mellow mahogany to exciting eucalyptus. Quality 25 inch solid-state color TV is built into your choice of two handsome fireplace consoles: traditional woodgrain look wall-mounted type with mantle, or contemporary freestanding metal hood type in persimmon enamel. High fidelity stereo sound for hissing embers or a roaring, crackling blaze. Remote control lets you vary flame color, brightness, contrast, and volume.

Mantel set: 695.95
Hood set: 629.95

Great American Scenes™
Photo Murals

A powerful interior design element that dramatically transforms any area; these lifelike giant color murals take you exciting places you may have missed (though they're right under your nose), and really bring home the experience. Quality of reproduction and brilliance of color make for highly graphic scenes that become the focus of attention, yet can just as easily recede into an unobtrusive background, depending on how you look at it.

Red Forest

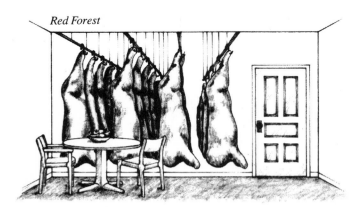

Red Forest

A rare look into a meat processing plant. Behold a refrigerated forest of tempting carcasses suspended like great edible stalactites from overhead racks and arrayed in long stately colonnades and aisles stretching as far as the eye can see. The foreground is so overpowering, you may not see the forest for the beef. Perfect for dining area.

Rolling Hills

Unless you look closely, this long shot of a garbage dump looks very much like a pleasant rural vista. The landscape of residential and industrial waste is being leisurely sculptured by several distant bulldozers, just like tractors working rich farmland. One can easily envision flocks and herds grazing peacefully on the delusive debris.

Slum Song

This tenement vignette is a surrealistic monochromatic composition of clotheslines, fire escapes, and bristling TV antennas poised over vacant canyons of broken glass and trash.

Cellblock Perspective

An inside look at a maximum security prison. A grid of vertical bars and endless horizontal mezzanines and railings extends into the distance, giving the illusion of space. Great for adding new dimension to a confined living area.

Next Window Please

The department of unemployment. A poignant panorama of frustration, shame, and rage, fading to an abstract pattern of long lines.

Tumbling Loads

The great American laundromat: a voyeur's delight.
You're on the outside looking into a steamy scene that
calls to mind post-impressionist compositions—a
swirling blur of intimate apparel.

Afterglow

An awesome look at the very heart of a nuclear power
plant—the throbbing reactor core. A great bundle of
fissionable fuel rods lurks beneath the surface of its
pool of heavy-water coolant like some menacing
mythological sea monster. Glows in the dark with an
eerie limelight. A dramatic mural for a bedroom.

Magic Markers

This sweeping vista of The National Cemetery for war
dead is an optical illusion: it looks like nothing more
than a geometric pattern of crisp white markers and
green lawn; you have to really squint to see it for
what it is.

All Great American Scenes™ Photo Murals are printed
on handsome suede finish vinyl. Scuff-resistant,
rugged, and scrubbable. Prepasted for application in
five easy pieces. 9x24 foot maximum wall size.
Request free color brochure. Each: 179.95

The Twenty Third Ham

The Lord is my swineherd; I shall not snort.
He maketh me to lie down in mud puddles.
He leadeth me beside swill waters.
His stores sell my soul.
He leadeth me in the path of oncoming cars
For his table's sake.
Yea, though I walk through the alley of the
    wholesale butcher,
I shall fear no cleaver.
For thou art museum.
Thy rod and thy staff infection.
They come for me.
Thou preparest a table from me
In the presence of thy inlaws.
Thou anointest my head with soy sauce;
My grease runneth over.
Surly sows and piglets will wallow with me
All the days in my sty,
And I will swell in the house of the hog forever.
Ah, ham.

Famous Fires™ Fireplace Logs

Nothing adds charm like a fire, and it's so easy with these fast-lighting logs of highest grade sawdust, paraffin, and unknown coloring agents. Choose from our *Urban Embers™* Series for a standard size log, and our new *Flames of Dissent™* Series of mini logs.

Urban Embers™ Logs

The great conflagrations of history captured in finely crafted and minutely detailed scale replicas: Rome 62 A.D., London 1666, Chicago 1871, and San Francisco 1906. Each city burns in color for up to three hours and ends in realistic ruins. The easy-lighting feature puts an end to false alarms. Important—do not remove wrapper when lighting; familiar skyline of city will emerge as flames engulf scene.

Individual City:	1.19
Carton of four identical Cities:	4.29
International Pack, four assorted Cities:	4.29

Rome, 62 A.D.

Flames of Dissent™ Mini-Logs

Scenes of personal tragedy from the lives of the best known heretics of history: Joan of Arc, Savonarola, and Giordano Bruno. These mini logs burn about an hour and a half—perfect when a large log is too much. The easy-lighting feature is built in to the dry twigs at base of stake to eliminate fussing and poking—just sit there and watch; scenes are graphic and historically faithful.

Individual Heretic:	.98
Three identical Heretics:	2.89
Three assorted Heretics:	2.89

Savonarola

Famous Fires™ Fireplace Logs are odorless and smokeless. They crackle like a real hardwood fire, but don't spit. Not for cooking. Do not move City or Heretic after lighting. Do not burn more than one City or Heretic at a time.

Measuring Up with Meat

A gram of ham = 0.035 ounces
A yard of lard = 0.914 meters
A pound of round = 0.454 kilograms
A peck of pork = 0.25 bushels
3 pig's feet = one barn yard
An ounce of prevention = a pound of cured ham

Bedbugs™ Sheets and Pillowcases

Luxurious linens with a design motif that really gets under your skin. Lounge amid a teeming riot of many different insect species. Bedbugs™ are so realistically depicted they almost seem to move—the total effect is a sea of twitching antennae and scurrying, darting forms. All the familiar household varieties are represented—ticks, chiggers, gnats, mites, fleas, silverfish and cockroaches—plus some exotic specimens like the spotted dunghopper, the toe louse, the armored carpet bug, the potato cicada, Asian thrips, the denture fly, the chattering corn borer, the star leech, and the sugardaddy-long-legs. Bedbugs™ biting realism is set against a background of earth tones, in no-iron poly/cotton percale.

Twin, flat or fitted:	11.95
Full or Queen, flat or fitted:	13.95
King, flat or fitted:	15.95
Standard Pillowcase:	2.95
King Pillowcase:	3.95

A Whole Whog™ Recipe: Pork Cheops

This proud platter is an all-pork tribute to the great Egyptian pharaoh Cheops, the builder of the loftiest of all the pyramids.

  1 whole ham, boned and rolled
  ½ cup honey
  1 cup brown sugar
  2 cloves
  3 lbs. bacon
  1 large pork sausage (8-10 inches)
  2 semicircular slices of pineapple
  1 orange segment
  2 shelled almonds
  1 bing cherry

Bake ham fat side up at 350° for 20 minutes per pound. Drain and skin. To glaze, paint with honey and sprinkle with brown sugar, then return to oven for ½ hour. Your ham is now ready to form the face of the pharaoh. Fashion the striped headdress with strips of bacon, using one strip for the rearing cobra over the brow. Cut a hole in the chin and insert the sausage to form the bound beard. Use the pineapple slices for ears, the cloves for nostrils, and the orange segment for the full, pursed lips. Almonds serve for the whites of the eyes; then press halved bing cherries in place for dark pupils.

The
Body
Shop

Oil of L.A.™

Oil of L.A.™ . . . the mysterious beauty fluid that forms an unseen smog-screen on your skin. It gives you relief from smog and other airborn irritants that can make you look years older. Oil of L.A.'s unique formula uses the principle of vaccination—actually refined from concentrated smog, it brings your body's own antibodies into play to build up a tolerance for killer smog. A rich and powerful emollient takes advantage of your body's moisture and penetrates quickly . . . while offering you constant protection from undesirable elements that lurk in the air. And remember, using Oil of L.A.™ reduces the amount of smog on the street—so help yourself to a lovelier you and you'll help L.A. too. Choose from three fragrances: "Freeway", "Motel", and new "Airport". For external use only. If swallowed do not induce vomiting. 4 ounces: 7.95

Hogwash™ Mouth Wash

Now neutralize sty breath, don't just cover it up. Refreshing pink pig-mint flavor won't discolor tongue. One quick swill-swish-and-spit in the morning protects you all day long. 24 ounce galvanized "watering trough" bottle: 2.99.

Asteroid Belt™ Trimmer

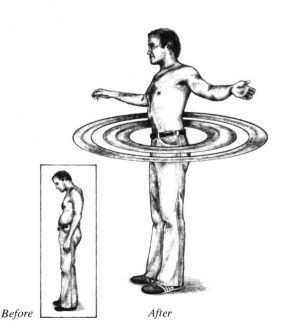

Before   *After*

Lose an unbelievable eight inches from waist and abdomen in less than 60 seconds. This mysterious belt of innumerable, small, kinetically-active particles lies somewhere between the solar plexus and pelvic girdle, capturing the power of distant stars and focusing it on you. Let the energy of outer space reduce your inner space. Melt inches away by redistributing bulk. No actual weight loss. No strenuous exercises. No dangerous diets. And no binding. Surround yourself with the ancient cosmic principle of non-expansion and watch it go to work for you instantly, tightening and trimming unsightly midriff bulge. Universal fit for all ages.   9.95

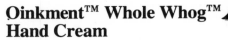

Oinkment™ Whole Whog™ Hand Cream

Cream yourself with this fast penetrating high friction moisturizer that never feels slippery on your hands. Hold anything firmly, even a greased pig. Now, without sacrificing proper hand care, you can get a grip on the job at hand—whether it's a golf club, tennis racquet, surgeon's scalpel, dentist's drill, or the steering wheel of an automobile or forklift. Don't risk costly errors in sports, embarrassing professional slipups during precision maneuvers, or dangerous lack of control while driving or operating machinery. 7 ounce pump-top "Pork Barrel" dispenser: 4.98

Braino™/Brainoff™ Stimulant/Sedative Set

Braino™

Opens closed thinking passages. Heightens perception and motor skills as it chews through blocks and flushes out stubborn resistance. Puts you on the alert—drive or operate machinery with confidence. Clears the way for effective goal orientation. Time-release action keeps passages open up to 12 hours for long lasting high performance. Warning: Product has reduced life-expectancy of laboratory animals, but specimens exhibit exceptional achievement level before succumbing. Not for children under four. High in polymers. 100 tablets in "green-light" traffic signal pillbox: 3.98

Brainoff™

Closes open thinking passages. Bans unwanted recurring thoughts and gently excludes disturbances and conflicting sensory data. Forms an invisible protective shield between you and the problem. Perfect for rationalization and procrastination. Reduces occasional panic and despair to manageable proportions and completely neutralizes minor anxiety and irritability. According to findings of a survey conducted by an accredited independent research organization, of all physicians asked, twice as many recommended the ingredient in Brainoff™ when used as directed than other leading stress control agents for helping to bring fast temporary relief of occasional minor symptoms of simple tension in actual clinical tests of effectiveness, as those who were not asked. Free of polymers. 100 tablets in "red-light" traffic signal pillbox: 3.98

Toilet Seatbelt

Don't get carried away on the toilet. This rugged seatbelt system employs over-the-shoulder harness plus lap belt to put an end to slipping and sliding. Cracks down even on severe forward thrust and side-sway to keep you sitting pretty. Avoid whiplash doo doo rear-end accidents. Don't fly off the handle when flushing. Boilable nylon webbing fights mold and mildew. Quick release buckles. Fits most standard bowls. Helmet not included. Void where prohibited.   27.98

The Blowhard™ Musical Blow Dryer

The wet-head is dead. This high performance unit combines a pro-power dryer/styler with a high fidelity audio tape player. While you blow dry you can play a repertoire of seven favorites: *Blowin' in the Wind, How Dry I Am, Stormy Weather, Blow the Man Down, Ill Wind, You Blow Me Away, Gone With the Wind*. Enjoy monaural listening through the high-output self-contained mini speaker or use the dual earplugs for stereo privacy. Quiet-flow fan will not drown out music. One-hand control for heat, flow, volume, treble, and bass. Energy-miser motor saves money—dry your hair for a song.   14.95

Neutron Balm

A highly effective topical balm which uses the body's own neutrons to neutralize minor local irritation without widespread side effects. Selective subatomic particles actually seek and destroy affected cell nuclei. Use this rash treatment to pinpoint trouble and nip it in the bud. Developed over years of radiotherapy research on laboratory specimens, this FDA approved formula is now available for general use. Provides a deterrent force against infection, and promotes natural radiance. Warhead flips its lid for easy dispensing. Note: before overall application, verify compatibility with body chemistry by testing on a small inconspicuous patch of skin. Warning: keep out of reach of children and unauthorized adults. Caution: contents under pressure; avoid rough handling. Six ounce vial: 2.95

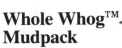

Whole Whog™ Mudpack

Let's face it, you're not going to be a piglet forever. Still, a sow can always look her best. She should never feel she has to hide her hide. Even if you wallow all day long your hide can dry out at night. Luxuriate in Whole Whog™ Mudpack all night long to restore vital moisture, help erase little lines around the snout, and tighten up bulges at the jowls and under the jaw. See results in just five overnight wallows and once again take pride in your hide. Ten-wallow mudpack pack:

7.95

Human Rainbow™ International Adhesive Bandages

Cover the wide spectrum of human skin when you get hurt. Human Rainbows™—the adhesive bandages in 20 colors—are your best camouflage, your best defense against infection, and your best buy. Pull off without pain. Easy pull-off pad won't sting your scab. Aids in healing. Aggressive adhesive sticks hard to skin, even when wet. Traditional shapes of Band, Patch, and Spot, plus five exciting new shapes: Shamrock, Pentagon, Spade, Star of David, Hammer and Sickle.

Pale Range	Yellow Range
Champagne Beige	Wild Ochre
Glazed Butterscotch	Jaundiced Half-and-Half
Rich Bisque	Bamboo Amber
Wet Putty	Pork Fried Rice
Blushing Buff	Mother of Pearl Harbor

Dark Range	Red Range
Raw Umber	Ready Red
Muted Umber	Berry Berry Red
Token Umber	English Not Red
Burnt Umber	No Reservations Red
Obsidian	Maize

Old World Pack. 500 Bands, one color, one shape: 7.95
New World Pack. 500 Bands, assorted colors
and shapes: 7.95

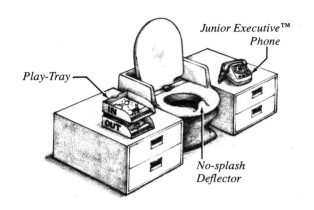

Junior Executive™
Phone

Play-Tray

No-splash
Deflector

Whole Whog™ Whiz Kid™ Potty Chair

The businesslike, intelligent way to ease your toddler's toilet training trauma. Start with the Whiz Kid™ and work up to the full sized commode. The Whiz Kid™ is the first potty chair with a brain. When baby hits pay dirt, unit automatically rewards him by reciting a poem through a hidden speaker: "This little piggy went wee-wee-wee all the way home." With self-cleaning vinyl seat, no-splash deflector, deodorizing lid, boilable chamber, and restraining strap. Junior Executive™ phone and play-tray keep underachievers busy while they sit it out.   49.95

Absorba the Greek™ Disposable Diapers

Pamper your toddler with mythical absorbancy in a classical form. Stay-dry flushable diapers in assorted color prints of ancient Greek motifs: choose from the Parthenon, the Trojan Horse, the Sack of Crete. Laurel scented. Developed and tested on Mediterranean infants. Unique capillary configuration gives greatest wicking action to fight diaper rash and chafing.

100 Newborn:	9.98
100 Toddler:	10.98
100 Overnight:	11.98

Pate Mate™ Pate Wax

Burning sun and drying wind can wreak havoc with a bald head. Protect that pate, and get sunscreen plus sheen with high-gloss Pate Mate™. Self-polishing action gives you a dazzling dome without tedious buffing. Black hat-brim scuff-marks wipe right off super hard surface. No yellow buildup. Great for noses too. Three ounces (about 10 coats):   3.95

Pig Iron™ Mineral Supplement

You're the active kind. You spend the day taking care of six little suckers, rooting for grubs, and stealing corn. But when evening rolls around you're always up for a robust wallow with your boar. You're no sallow sow. You keep that rosy hue in your cheeks. You keep your hide firm and your snout moist. You take Pig Iron™... every day. Pig Iron™ delivers nearly twice the iron of ordinary mineral supplements—it's a hard fact that won't let you go soft. So to be your best, take care of yourself: eat right, get the rest, and take Pig Iron™... every day. Tablet and liquid.   3.95

Self-Propelled Cane

Eliminate the bump and grind of conventional canes. Now you can have needed support without creating friction. Just guide and go—the lightweight rechargeable electric motor is good for six average walks. No more power cord trailing behind you. And no more fatigue caused by cane use on uneven terrain; four-wheel drive pushes through even gross irregularities to give you the right of way.   79.95

A Whole Whog™ Easy Holiday Snack: "Walloween" (Trick or) Treats

Just press a pink candy-coated almond into the hole of a mini chocolate-covered donut and you've got a piglet wallowing in a mud puddle to treat your little neighborhood tricksters.

Denture Adhesives

A poor seal is no laughing matter. Clamp down on slipping and sliding for a song. Stick 'em up without putting the bite on your budget. Choose from powders, sprays, or cements. All only 98¢.

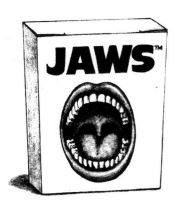

Jaws™

Awesome holding power. Won't let loose under pressure. Even tackles very rare meat. Food will never again give you the slip. No fishy odor.

Plate Mate™

An accommodating gum buddy that molds to your every contour. Gives you a fit like hand in glove. Knows its place and won't try to slip out the side.

Gum Job™

As an overdoer, you've got a big job—you're up against some mighty powerful roughage. But you've got a powerful friend: high-tack Gum Job™ forms a heavy-duty gasket that stands up to the task at hand. It even handles corn. There's no job that doesn't come in its grip.

Chicken Gumbo™

An original old Creole formula that works gently and naturally. Uses your body's own chicken to prevent runaway plates.

Tongue-in-Cheek™

For the socially active denture wearer of any age. With built-in deodorant you're set for public speaking or an intimate caucus. High holding power for plates that take a beating more from suction than impact. Get as close as you want without fear of a slip-up. Hold tight all night.

Food Man Chew™

An inscrutable oriental adhesive with an ancient herbal formula. Never loses its grasp of the larger context and thereby is able to treat the Whole Whog™.

Bridge Over Troubled Waters™

Prevents catastrophic structural failures in public. Spans trouble spots to get you over precarious pitfalls of mastication.

Family Colonic Irrigation System

Family regularity runs in cycles—now and then everybody is caught between a rock and a hard place at the same time. That's when this hospital-tested irrigator comes to the rescue. Inspired by the multiple-tube oriental hookah pipe, it has many outlets so there's no waiting. Family members can plug in for simultaneous relief and everyone has an outlet. Large capacity and no-leak close-tight bottleneck.

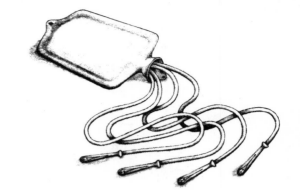

4 outlet unit for small nuclear family: 7.95
8 outlet unit for large nuclear family: 12.95
16 outlet unit for stem family: 22.95

The Grabber™ Nonskid Soap

The National Safety Board and The President's Council on Lavatory Safety agree: most home accidents involving catastrophic injury are caused by a fall in the tub or shower due to conventional slippery soap. Prevent potential tragedy—put The Grabber™ in your tub. Its special formula has thousands of tiny tentacles to cling tight wherever you put it down. You can even park it on your body when not in use. The cake won't pull off, but it releases with a gentle side-to-side motion such as used in lathering.
Jumbo cake: .89

Hypno-pot-o-mist™

The two-way vaporizer for both respiration and meditation. Hypno-pot-o-mist™ opens you up whether the block is nasal or mental. Blow your mind *and* your nose. A mini mesopotamian hippopotamus lurks beneath rubber lotus pads in a pot of water; occasionally he surfaces, yawns, and blows off steam. Frequency of hippo's appearance is variable. The effect is hypnotic. Great for séances—creates an occult cloud-cover for atmosphere. Use as a humidifier to come through a long hard winter in comfort, without family members drying up.   23.95

Red sky at morning, hogs take warning;
red sty at night, butcher's delight.

Food in Your Hair

Your hair can't survive on egg, beer, and milk alone. Hair needs a balanced, well-rounded diet; it has its own individual appetite. There may be certain favorite foods it can't do without. Choose from this banquet of hair nutriments and be sure your hair isn't going hungry.

Pasta Plus™ Shampoo

Lots of protein and fatty acids are great, but don't forget the carbohydrates. Active hair needs food to burn, so don't starve it—pile on the pasta, and add body to thin and lifeless hair by giving it the essential starch it craves. 3.79

Cottage Cheese 'n' Celery™ Conditioner

Hair can have *too much* body. That's when you need a diet conditioner to gently strip away excess body that can cause overstuffed, portly, full-figured, or heavy-set hair. ·2.89

Poi 'n' Soy™ Grooming Aid

A juicy snack-food for dry and frizzy hair. Watch parched shafts drink up the moisture and lie down satisfied. 3.98

Crumbled Egg and Caviar Hollandaise

Hair that's a fussy eater deserves the best. Give gourmet hair the luxury of this incomparable caviar conditioning shampoo. There's egg for protein and luster—separate the whites from the yolks. Finish with a tingling champagne rinse. Go whole hog . . . because you're worth it. 49.95

Touch of Ratatouille™

Damage can be done if hair is teased or ratted too much. Apply first-aid with this delicately simmered vegetable conditioner pack that restores integrity with its edible complex of vitamins. The perfect treatment for stripped hair: rich lather penetrates deep into the hair follicle to promote a natural balance; then it rinses clean and leaves no film. 3.49

Jiggle™ Quick-Setting Gel

This festive dessert of shimmering gelatin with suspended fruit is a quick fix to put the bounce back in a set that's gone limp. 3.49

Meal-at-a-Glance™

Your hair needs at least one balanced meal every day, and here it is: start with an endive salad heat-pack scalp treatment; for a shampoo entree try the filet of swan with truffle sauce and broccoli au gratin; then move on to the rich chocolate mousse conditioner. Top it off with a heady coffee liqueur rinse.   39.95

Suppository Key Fob

In a bind? Spending the night out? Introducing the suppository that's always there when you need it in a pinch. Whether you want a laxative *or* a contraceptive, help is never farther away than your keys. Special dual-purpose formula withstands high pocket temperatures without melting—always stays firm for easy insertion. Easy-open bubble pack. Eight suppository fobs plus ring: 3.95. Keys not included.

Dental Floss Sweater

At a loss without floss? Never be without dental floss again. Here's a lifetime supply* that you can actually wear. Fight plaque and tartar in full-fashioned easy-care knits for all members of the family. To use, unravel collar, sleeves, or waist. Special knit resists accidental or compulsive unravelling. Miniature molar emblem replaces the familiar alligator. Waxed or plain in turquoise (spearmint flavor), crimson (cinnamon), or sienna brown (beef flavor). Will not pill, matt, ball, shed, or frizz. Do not iron. State gender, color, flavor, and size.   19.95

*Based on current statistics of the American Dental Association for per capita floss use, and of the U.S. Census Bureau for average life span. Your actual lifetime may vary.

A Whole Whog™ Pork Tip

Tight lock? Just dip your key in bacon fat for easy insertion. Will not stain pocket.

Anti-Perspirants

Choosing an anti-perspirant—and having to pick your way through a jungle of forms and features to find the combination that's right for you—is enough to make you work up a sweat. Find relief in this selection, which contains many traditional possibilities plus a few new ones.

Nozone™

A wetness fighting aerosol spray for use when ease of application takes precedence over environmental considerations. Discreet package looks like a roll-on. New, lighter formula contains less of those substances said to harm the ozone. Even excessive doses have *not* caused cancer in laboratory animals (although suffocation has sometimes resulted).   1.95

Arm Candy™

A fine white powder spray that works overtime to keep up with you. Easy to take; never wet, brown, or gummy. Also a great nasal decongestant. Non-aerosol. No stain, no sting.   29.95

Gland Plus™

The thick stick that stands up to wetness but knows how to be gentle on your skin. No tedious pumping. Screw-up dispenser. Anti-stain solid.   1.89

Young, Gifted, and Dry™

Extra heavy duty formula roll-on for the prodigal performing artist. Precision-fit ball will not snag hair. Neutral, natural, or unscented.   1.79

The Sting™

If you think it has to hurt to help, this effective spray is for you. Smarting pinpoints the treated area; no more guessing where you've covered.   1.98

Morning Arm™

Not just a one night stand. The strongest long-lasting solid. Won't run out on you during the night. There to protect you in the morning. Wake up secure and feeling fresh.   1.69

Whisper™

The first talking deodorant, this roll-on actually tells you when you are about to offend. Contains a special expiration-indicator substance which emits a quiet warning hiss half an hour before complete breakdown of effectiveness.   1.59

The Wart Hog™ Wart Remover

Plagued by warts? Now you can get rid of unsightly warts safely and painlessly at home. This ingenious device, which looks like a whimsical wart hog, is a surgical quality wart remover. The tail dispenses a drop of topical anesthetic, the razor-sharp jaws snip wart cleanly, and the tusks cauterize. Rechargeable—does up to 30 warts on one charge.   49.95

Cauterizer

Anesthetic Dispenser

Snipper

Vitamin B-1 Bomber

The fun and easy way for kids to take their B vitamins. (Fun for parents too.) Scale model of the scrapped B-1 Bomber is a dispenser stocked with "bomb" capsules, each containing 100% of the RDA of vitamin B-1. Child lies face up on "ground zero" with mouth open, and parent plays bombardier from above. Blast malnutrition and zero in on family health while you share in the suspense and excitement of a simulated nuclear strike. Add to the realism with the Air Force officer's cap and "wings" lapel pin for parent, and full-face masks for child which are topographical color reproductions of three actual military-industrial targets: steel mill, oil refinery, guerrilla sanctuary.

Plane, 100 Bombs, Hat, Wings, 3 Map Masks: 11.98
100 Bomb Refill Pack: 2.49

Magic Pill Wand

Cast a spell while you pop a pill. Make that wish come true with this magic wand that is an enchanting dispenser for tablets and capsules. A brisk wave of the wand activates release of antibiotics, birth control, and stress control, as well as recreational drugs. New two-way release: "drop" (gravity release), and "pop" (horizontal ejection). Built-in counter and frequency governor prevent abuse. 100 pill capacity. Brushed chrome staff, bright brass star. With book of spells and wishes.   19.95

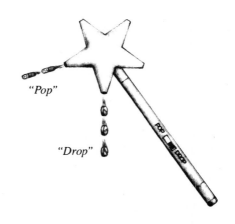

"Pop"

"Drop"

Julienne Seizure Salad

Embarrassed by spasms and convulsions? Now you can carry fast relief in discreet salad form. Powerful medicine is cleverly concealed in this appetizing mini-gourmet Caesar salad which is a tribute to the great epileptic emperor. A centerpiece of savory julienne-style carrots nestles in a bed of Romaine lettuce drenched in egg yolk and sprinkled with seasoned croutons and plump kidney beans. Handy leakproof half-pint take-out food container. No mail orders. 4.95

Bust Developers

Don't fall flat where it counts most. Shape up. Dare to stand out and make your point with one of these three great developers. Today's revealing fashions demand it.

Mammorex™

Is it you, or is it Mammorex™? It's you! This unique pectoral pumper is also a fine quality concertina. You don't just pump; you make music at the same time, so the exercise is easier to take. Play just five songs a day and see shattering results in two weeks with strengthened pectoral muscles for greater uplift. 179.95

Mammorex™

Tut's Pyramids™

Put the mysterious power of the pyramid to work for you while you sleep. No exercises. Just put pair in place and let stand overnight. Harness the force of the pharaohs and focus it on *you* to actually stimulate cell growth. Don't be a slave to heredity. Undo the curse of the mummy, and experience the fullness thereof when your cup runneth over. You'll have them licking their Cheops. 12.99

Hope Chest™

For the 12–15 set. Remember the myth of Pandora's Box: when all else escapes you there's still hope. Now you can turn that hope chest into a treasure chest with easy exercises involving body postures and manipulation of the lid of the box. Wake up stunted growths and gently encourage sluggish or retarded development. 4.95

Whole Whog™ Scents

Make a selection from this collection of alluring fragrances. Make the statement that's exactly right, be it a subtle snort, or a show-stopping squeal.

Hog Wild™

A joyous, impetuous, and uninhibited scent. A touch at the nostrils, a touch behind the hocks . . . and you may just start a stampede!   7.95

Swamp Gas™

A devious and overpowering knockout of a body mist. This dense fragrance doesn't linger in the air. It hugs the ground, sneaks up on him . . . and it's all over.   8.95

Pink Aura™

Sensual, yet ethereal, with a touch of innocence. A halo of subtle quintessence stays very much with you as you plow through your day.   11.95

Tusk, Tusk™

Dusky and untamed, this toothsome fragrance is an irresistible hog call that makes its point loud and clear. Use this legendary aphrodisiac and you'll have a bristling wild boar on your hands. Distinctive eight ounce mister: 9.95

Eau de Porc™

Captivatingly continental. Refined yet candid. An aroma that reacts with individual body chemistry— different on each sow who wallows in it. The cologne that sets you apart from the rank and file of the sty.   15.95

A Whole Whog™ Limerick: Big City Sow

There once was a sow who aspired
to be daintily groomed and attired;
so she painted her snout
and she decked herself out,
but got characteristically mired.

Apparel:
Intimate
and Otherwise

Braille Bra

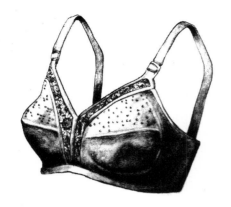

Your blind date gets the message. Braille excerpts from *The Kama Sutra* and *The Song of Solomon* are embossed around outside of cups. Deep-plunge front with bias-cut crossover flatters you, molds you, shapes you, moves with you, and gives both of you a lift. Cups are lined with an ever-so-subtle layer of soft spun fiberfill to add a little you that only you will know about. Lacy triacetate cups, stretch spandex side panels, and adjustable nylon tricot straps. Cushioned underwire won't pinch or dig. Challenging four-hook back closure. White, nude, salmon. 32-42, AA-DD.   17.95

Bible Belt

Gird your loins with the grace of God, ward off satanic forces, and reinforce your sagging faith with this spiritually uplifting Bible Belt. One size fits all believers—there's always enough to go around. Belt is of top grain sacrificial lambhide with hand-tooled embossed scenes from both Old and New Testaments including the plague of boils, the scourge of Sodom and Gomorrah, Jacob wrestling with the angel, Lazarus rising from the dead, and Jesus sitting on his ass. Brass-look buckle is the tablets of the ten commandments, mounted upside-down for easy reading by the wearer.   29.95

Dominant™ Jeans

Assert your right to make a definitive statement and come on strong. Beat the pecking order and really stand out in front in these sleek jeans that are styled for your mature body. Full fitted padded crotch, snug thighs, and slight seat uplift. High-rise waist with fast-release clasp and smooth-action brass fly. Dark indigo. 90% cotton, 10% unknown fibers.   49.95

A Whole Whog™ Ham Hint:
Ham in a Hammock

Here's a festive foundation for your next glazed ham. Weave strips of bacon into a "hammock" in an oval serving platter. Then bring on the ham, lower away, and enjoy.

Solar Bowler

Tip your hat to the sun and kiss fossil fuels goodbye. You're ahead of your time with the Solar Bowler—a lightweight hat collector that takes charge fast for personal electric power. Continental flare and solar flare come together on your head to set you off as one conservative of energy. Provides a convenient outlet for personal power—a portable plug-in for electric shaver, power toothbrush, heating pad, trouble light, vibrator, etc. Runs personal appliances such as timepieces, hearing aids, and pacemakers without batteries. (Recommended for use with pacemakers in Florida and Arizona only.) Qualify for IRS tax credit (Form 4492, "Credits for Energy-Efficient Apparel").   89.95

Whole Whog™ T-Shirts

Get it on and get it off your chest. Make your statement in comfortable and long-wearing cotton-blend crew-neck T-shirts from Whole Whog™:

Go Whole Whog™　　　　　*Missing Link*
High on the Hog　　　　　*Make Mine Meat*
Pig Latin Lover　　　　　*Save the Bones*
Smoked Hams Last Longer　*Get Off on Jerkey*

White lettering and trim on bacon-brown shirt. State size. For boars and sows as well as piglets.
Single shirt: 8.95
Whole Whog™ Assortment of 8 shirts   69.95

Muffler Briefs

The great barrier brief. A double-acting brief that serves as both an auditory and an olfactory shield. Put the damper on embarrassing flatulence. Eradicate erratic eructations. Shock absorbing design curtails kickback. No offensive buffeting or vibration. Three-day disposable filter bag. Don't hold back. *You're* under pressure?—*Our* underwear!
3 Briefs, 24 Filter Bags: 19.95

Too many hogs spoil the trough.

Legal Briefs

Hold up in court. The appealing way to drive home your point, these briefs are printed with condensed texts of landmark decisions of the Supreme Court. Triple-stretch cotton/poly blend stands up under intense cross-examination. Settle for less and court disaster. Witness this marriage of durability and comfort, and you be the judge. Don't condemn yourself to binding arbitration—rest your case. It's evident that Legal Briefs are your best defense. You'll swear by them.

Pair o' Legal Briefs (trial offer):	1.95
Briefs in triplicate:	3.95
Nine briefs in the "Don't Get Court Short" Briefcase:	14.95

Suburban Turban

Here's a heady cover-up inspired by the passion and bravado of Islam. Curb a flyaway coif or keep curlers under cover while shopping. The biggest curlers get the widest coverage. Take over, hold that unruly hair hostage, and come out ahead. Top it all off by going in circles with yards of diaphanous chintz that never comes to a point.   9.95

Silver Chicken Boa

Inspired by the whole-skin silver fox fur boas of the forties (with the heads intact), and in keeping with the look of revival elegance, we proudly offer this trio of magnificent Rhode Island Red cocks. A fashion coup of roosters that will really wake up the pecking order; there's no telling what a cocky dude'll do. The three form a ring—beak to talon and talon to beak—to encircle you with the impeccable luxury of real chicken. Urban dwellers who have never witnessed the splendor of these creatures in their natural unplucked state will be stunned by the sensuous downy softness of the feathers. Their snowy opalescence is reminiscent of the incomparable aura of the silver fox. A brilliant scarlet comb, real bloodstone eyes, and lacquered beaks and talons add the exotic finishing touches. Guaranteed not endangered.   49.95

Leisure Wet Suit

This handsomely tailored leisure suit is equally at home on land or in the water. Traditional polyester foamfill double knit burgundy blazer sports white topstitching, deep center vent, and waterproof pockets. Flared slacks in lime and canary check pattern with white leather-look polyurethane weight belt. Reversible ruffle-front rubber dickey in solid lime or canary is coordinated to slacks. Black vinyl bow tie. White vinyl flippers with stay-on elastic insteps. White face mask. High glare sharkskin-finish serves as an example to sharks and keeps them at a distance. Sleek surface will not snag on jagged coral branches. Full terry-lined for underwater comfort. True wash-and-wear action: washes itself as you wear it; then tumble dry on shore. Lean cut, full, regular, or porcine. State waist and inseam. Breathing gear not included.   89.95

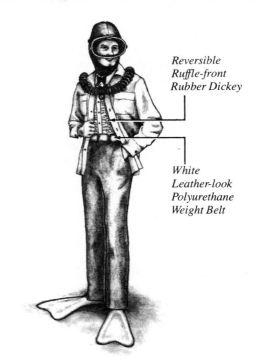

*Reversible
Ruffle-front
Rubber Dickey*

*White
Leather-look
Polyurethane
Weight Belt*

Executive Economic-Indicator Tie

A great gift item—now there's no longer any need to worry that it's trite to give a tie. The Executive Economic-Indicator Tie turns red to indicate a troubled economy and black to indicate a healthy one. Just input current levels of gross national product, Dow Jones, prime rate, unemployment rate, wholesale price index —and tie does the rest. Mini memory chips woven throughout tie electro-chemically activate red or black pigments impregnated in fabric fibers to indicate the state of the nation's economy in a simple straightforward way, without giving you a lot of conflicting and ambiguous data and leaving you hog-tied about what it all means. Make financial decisions with confidence. Programmable by simple hookup to any calculator keyboard. When tie is not indicating, the "business as usual" pattern of diagonal gray and ochre stripes reappears to complement any suit.   29.95

Let sleeping hogs lie.

Objets
d'Art

Jawbone-of-an-Ass Nutcracker

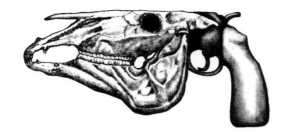

Stubborn nuts? Break through those hard shells with the real thing—a limited-edition jawbone of an ass from the government-sanctioned thinning of the donkey population in the Grand Canyon. (Includes copy of U.S. Forest Service permit.) A conversation piece for your coffee table, as well as an efficient nutcracker: long leverage and nature's own geometry make it easy to use. Crack two nuts at once—one on each side. All molars are intact, but some front teeth may be missing. Stainless steel hinge. Steam cleaned for your protection.   79.95

Toot Uncommon™

Those of discriminating taste know that now and then you have to turn your nose up at some things and insist on the genuine article. It is for them that we offer this uncompromising miniature ornamental coffin container and dispenser. Unlike the spate of imitations, this piece is superbly crafted in the actual materials of the original: pure beaten gold, lapis lazuli, obsidian, and inlaid turquoise. Apply pressure on a secret spot and the boy-king flips out to reveal a silver spoon attached to his face and the "toot suite" inner chamber to safely stash the remains of *your* treasure. A royal comfort in this life or the next. We ask that hereafter customers order by mail or phone only—because of the recent unprecedented demand—and do not come to our distribution center. No lines and no waiting. (Hand shown not included.)   3998.95

The Ten Canned Ham Hints

I   Thou shalt have no other hogs before me.
II   Thou shalt not make thine own gravy.
III   Thou shalt not shoot thyself in vein.
IV   Remember the bloodbath and keep it at bay.
V   Honor thy fodder and thy mudder.
VI   Thou shalt not swill.
VII   Thou shalt not commit animal husbandry.
VIII Thou shalt not squeal.
IX   Thou shalt not wear false eyelashes.
X   Thou shalt not covet thy neighbor's ass.

Insects of America
Thimble Collection

The beauty of the insect microcosm has long held a fascination for mankind. The specimens that frequent our gardens and campgrounds provide a never-ending source of delight and wonder with their uncanny behavior and appearance. Now The American Entomological Society, in conjunction with the *Whole Whog Catalog,* proudly invites you to acquire this exquisite limited-edition collection of traditional decorated thimbles inspired by the insects of America. We have painstakingly captured twelve favorite members of the miniature kingdom in tiny and delicate thimbles of finest bone china. The high glaze and milky translucency of bone china are the perfect setting for the consummate artisty of the celebrated illustrator and distinguished entomologist, Beatrice Beebe. With profusion of color and precision of line she has created a masterpriece of breathtaking realism in these specially commissioned miniatures. Thrill to the sight of the Blue-Tailed Dragonfly, body aglow with fiery highlights of turquoise iridescence, her delicate gossamer wings poised for balance as she releases her slippery load of shimmering pearly pupae into the deep recesses of a fresh carcass. Here is the Praying Mantis, tiny tyrannosaurus of the grass, locked in mortal combat with a Boll Weevil and deftly avoiding the Weevil's formidable pincers as he crushes her head in his powerful mandibles. And marvel at the drama of the Black Widow Spider as she stings and paralyzes a male she has just mated with, and begins to wrap him up for later digestion with glistening silken cords secreted from a special gland in her abdomen. This captivating collection will prove to be a joy to own, to display, and to pass down through generations. Subscribe now to the set of twelve thimbles, sent monthly, at only 9.95 each. Elegant hardwood display case included.

A Whole Whog™ Haiku

Lazy summer day.
Cornfed porkers loll in their wallow
amid guttural grunts of contentment.
Nearby the butcher sharpens his cleaver.

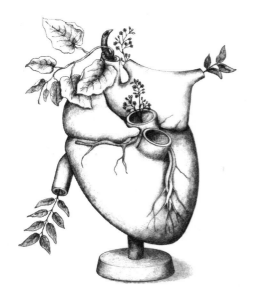

Heart Transplanter

A stroke of genius. The human heart supplies the perfect shape for this starter-planter for herbs and spices that will later be transplanted into larger pots. Young shoots love to nestle in the sheltered chambers and to peek out of the open stubs of veins and arteries as they reach out into the light. The finely crafted ceramic heart with anatomically correct detail is actual size, skillfully hand painted in living color. An extra thick high-gloss glaze simulates the heart's own shimmering *pericardium* covering. The interior is correctly divided into four chambers so you can plant four tiny crops and keep them apart. Water from above through either the *inferior vena cava* or the *pulmonary vein.* And don't worry about root-rot. If you accidentally overwater, the Coronary Bypass™ automatically channels the excess directly to the *aorta,* which ascends to the *left ventricle* to expedite drainage. With six ounce bottle of Pace-Maker™ concentrate to regulate growth rate.   49.95

Sperm Whale   *Killer Whale*

Gray Whale   *Right Whale*

Prints of Whales

The royalty of the seas make their mark with this limited edition of actual prints of the blow-holes of four of the most distinguished whale members: the sleek Killer Whale, the gentle Gray Whale, the frisky Sperm Whale, and the mighty Right Whale. Save them. The original direct impression is painstakingly reproduced in fine lithographs to accurately render all the intricate tracery of line in each giant kiss. Display and cherish these masterpieces for years to come. Includes Certificate of Authenticity (also suitable for framing). Four prints 18x18: 89.95. Order now and receive an exciting bonus gift for just 1.99—*Songs of Whales* stereo record or cassette—actual wailing set to favorite selections including:

Splish Splash
Twist and Spout
Bleat of the Deep
Beached Baby Blues
Our Love is a Fluke of Nature
When the Harpoon Comes Over the Mountain
Green Dolphin Street
The Devil or the Deep Blue Sea Blue Whale Blues
Blubber Come Back

Interstate Highway Signs
Charm Bracelet

The excitement of America's main arteries—our major Interstate Highways—is captured in these ten exquisitely wrought gold filled authentic miniature road sign charms. The familiar shield symbol is emblazoned with those magic numbers that conjure up exotic faraway places.Experience the romance and adventure of 90, the gentle beauty of 5, the historic enchantment of 95, the challenging ordeal of 80, the incomparable austere grandeur of 40, and more. 24.95

Nuclear Sub
Commemorative Gravy Boat

Next time you make gravy, commemorate the tragic sinking of the nuclear submarine USS *Thresher*. This traditional pewter gravy boat has a surprise inside— a finely crafted scale replica of the *Thresher*, lying helplessly on its side at the bottom, just like the original. The hollow sub is stockpiled with a richly seasoned concentrated mushroom powder—when hot liquid strikes it, a savory mushroom cloud explodes in your gravy. Gravy Boat, 12 Mushroom-Cloud Fuel Pellets: 19.95

The Poem on the Statute of Limitations

Give me your sow and your boar,
Your huddled masses yearning to breed free,
No wretched refuse from the butcher's floor,
Send these, the boneless tempting cuts to me—
I lift my ham beside the oven door.

Social
Security
Systems

Suburban Scarecrows

A good scarecrow is an economical alternative to sophisticated electronic security systems. These amazingly lifelike mannikins really work to outwit burglars. Set consists of an entire inflatable family: 2 parents, 2 children, one grandparent, and the family dog. Set them all up in the living room with lights and TV on, put the dog on the front lawn, and leave the house. Make different scenes to keep burglars guessing; flexible joints allow you to reposition the family at will. Kiss 'n' Blo™ patented filler valve is concealed in mannikin's mouth. (Or for quick fill, use blow dryer, holding the figure's lips snugly around the nozzle.) This scarecrow family has many other uses: save seats in theaters and places in line; prevent auto break-ins by leaving the dog on the back seat; when you drive downtown take the grandparent along plus a wheelchair (not included) for special handicapped parking privileges; when commuting by car take any two figures along to qualify for carpool toll discount. Each suburban scarecrow shrinks to the size of a rubber glove, and the entire deflated family stores in shoebox or glove compartment.   129.95

Kiss 'n' Blo™
Patented Filler System

Guard Hog

Don't live in fear. Enjoy the security and peace of mind that accompany owning an attack animal. Protect your family, home, and business with this ferocious wart hog that's trained to charge unauthorized personnel. The mere sight of a full-grown charging wild boar, with its grotesque warts, savage expression, and flashing tusks is enough to discourage any intruder. Good with children. Certified housebroken. No mail orders. 349.95. Or bring your own piglet to us for training.

Many important telephone calls are missed because the receiver is off the hook. Make sure business associates and loved ones can reach you—hang up carefully and securely. Place the receiver firmly and accurately in place, then release your grip by straightening *all* fingers and remove your hand *completely* before turning away to leave the area.

The Nuke Nook

Nuclear nuisance? Don't over-react in your con-fusion. Take refuge in the Nuke Nook, the portable inflatable fallout shelter for the entire nuclear family. Get fast relief from dangerous radiation levels whether caused by neighborhood reactor failure or by act of war. Nook monitors the air and automatically inflates when there's trouble. Made of durable plutonium/polyester blend, the fashionable fissionable material with the long half-life. Impervious and leakproof. Won't melt down when the heat's on. Bread and water not included.

389.95

The Browbeater™
Digital Courtesy Cap

Tired of the perfunctory protocol of social situations? Here's a long-needed device to streamline the tedious litany of "Thank you—You're welcome" and "Sorry —It's all right" without being vague and without sacrificing credibility. The large easy-read LED electronic display flashes one of these four common messages plainly across your brow at a touch of the remote pocket controller. The display may be silent, or may be accompanied by a male or female voice or by an electronic beep. Flash your message briefly as needed during transient social intercourse or display it constantly for ongoing social postures. For even greater freedom switch mode from Manual to Auto-reciprocation, and your cap will interface with any other cap within a ten foot radius so that all units automatically respond with the appropriate display— "Thank you" elicits "You're welcome", and "Sorry" elicits "It's all right" (the less common "Not at all" and "Think nothing of it" are also available); you don't even have to pay attention. A great gift idea—watch your grateful recipient flash his first "Thank you". Cap is of metallic polyurethane; in silver, bronze, copper, platinum, or zinc.

79.95

The Hothead™
Telephone Ear Conditioner

They can bend your ear, but they can't burn it. Hold the line against ear discomfort and prevent heat rash on marathon calls. Even cools conference calls. The Hothead™ mini air conditioner mounts unseen inside phone earpiece. Silent and unheard of. Thermostatic control adjusts to the heat of your ear. When the heat's on, just dial to your favorite listening temperature.

59.95

Fallout Fez

Safe   *Contaminated*

An attractive traditional Middle-Eastern fez with a built-in mini Geiger counter, which indicates the presence of radioactivity by spinning the fez's tassel around in a circle: slow rotation for low levels, and fast spin for dangerous levels. Warns you of radiation in your surroundings and warns others if *you* are contaminated. Adjustable calibration for changing the safe level. (To determine safe level subtract 50% from government recommendation.) Fez is of slippery 100% rayon so that fallout falls off. The no-hassle tassel is machine washable.   99.95

Foreclosure Door Closer

This proven security measure is a real setback to intruders who get their foot in the door. Originally developed to ward off home foreclosures, unit works equally well against repossession, collection, eviction, and routine sales efforts. Sudden heavy pressure from outside of door activates switch, and powerful hydraulic action closes door instantly, against even the most stubborn resistance. Spare yourself the embarrassment of ugly scenes caused by pushy intruders. Keep your home a safe and secure sanctuary. With special scoop-shaped strip that clips to outside bottom edge of door to prevent foot injury to intruder, which could result in additional legal action. Install without tools or instructions.   89.95

You're Welcome Notes

Daisy

Push politeness to its limit and emphasize your appreciation for a thank-you note. Go out of your way and show this special consideration to someone who was nice enough to remember to express gratitude for a thoughtful gesture on your part. Choice of five designs: *Sunset, Daisy, Lightning Bolt, Rainbow,* and *Wistful Frog.* 100 Notes plus envelopes: 2.79

No-Guest Strip

At last an easy answer to persistent guest problems. This double-acting guest-repellant strip rids home of unwanted visitors *and* prevents future infestation. Gives you up to 90 days of freedom from unwelcome guests. Stand, hang, or stick up in area where guests congregate, and a powerful yet safe formula goes to work emitting a sub-threshold odor to make guests and would-be guests leave without knowing why. No more tiresome and embarrassing direct confrontations. Works even on stubborn guests. (Family members experience a mild vague uneasiness for several hours, but then get used to it.) Control guests in homes, apartments, condominiums, cabins, campers, wherever there is a guest problem. Even works outdoors in gardens and patios—steady and compelling action is unaffected by wind and weather. Non-toxic for most pets. Solid enclosed odor cake in reclosable unit with adjustable vents—partly open to reduce guest activity; full open to eliminate it entirely. No assembly required.   3.95

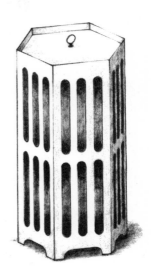

Smile Magnifier

Make a larger than life impression and give new dimensions to your personality. This dual purpose unit magnifies both smiles and frowns to enlarge your powers of both persuasion and coercion. Broaden your appeal, add clout to your administrative ability, heighten your charisma, and generally enhance your credibility. Switch on the built-in illuminator to emphasize your intentions with dramatic lighting (batteries not included). Great for high-stress situations, public speaking, fund-raising, etc. Also perfect for speaking to the deaf—shows large, easy to read lips. Lens swings up over head when not in use to allow for eating, drinking, or normal speech. (Warning: Not for prolonged use in direct sunlight; focusing property of lens may cause third degree facial burns.)   14.99

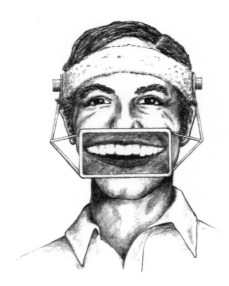

Creation
and Recreation

Chatty Freudy Doll™

Toddler trauma? Kids can't cope? Here's a toy that's not just educational, but positively therapeutic. Inscrutable psychoanalyst doll converses with child, and does a lot more listening than talking. He nods and says "uh-huh...I see...go on" every 30 seconds, then resumes his characteristic faraway look. Flashing light and buzzer indicate end of session. Use payment slot (takes bills only) to start new session. With four costumes and four mini backdrops. Costumes: three-piece suit for practice, white lab coat for research, tweed jacket and slacks for teaching, and playsuit for lounging at home. Backdrops: office, clinic, university lecture hall, and living room. Detachable easy-clean goatee.   19.95

Puppet Government Set

Set the stage for an exciting political drama with an entire government of puppets: a Premier, 2 Generals, 4 Loyalist Troops, 2 Foreign Advisors, 1 Multinational Corporation Representative, 1 Guerrilla Leader, 3 Guerrilla Troops, and 6 Civilians. Maneuver your characters in four miniature sets: Conference Room, Street Demonstration, Guerrilla Bunker, and Palace Coup. Act out a complex intrigue of secret deals, covert operations, and arms sales. You manipulate puppets unseen from above to give the appearance of independent movement. Many strings attached for highly articulate control. Follow one of the three standard scripts included, or create your own twists of dramatic development. With stage, puppeteer blind.   119.95

Tranquillizer Darts

Discover the soothing fun of darts. This unusual set features three well balanced syringe darts and a giant pill board that's divided into only two sections—easy on your eyes and easy to score. Low-key play dispels anxieties. Tow the line, hit the spot, and win occasional temporary relief. Come away hero or heroine. Even losers get some relief from the hypnotic effect of concentrating on the target. Win or lose, this game keeps you coming back for more.   24.95

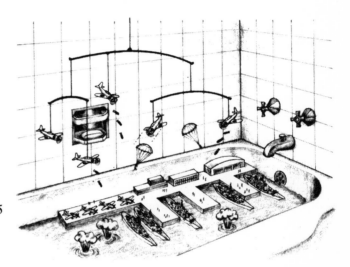

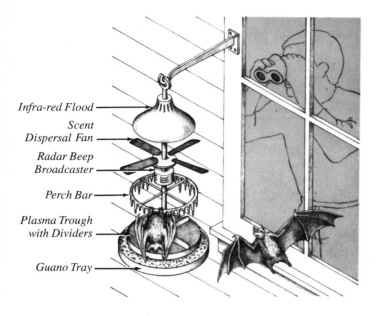

Infra-red Flood

Scent
Dispersal Fan

Radar Beep
Broadcaster

Perch Bar

Plasma Trough
with Dividers

Guano Tray

The Batmobile™ Bat Feeder

Many people are finding bats more interesting to watch than hummingbirds, and this unit really brings home the bats. Hang outside window and bats will soon appear. They land and dangle from the circular perch bar while they feed on cow plasma in a trough below them. The built-in fan disperses the plasma scent to attract bats within a five mile radius; then during their final approach the ultrasonic beep broadcaster gives bat's radar the exact location of feeder to prevent landing collisions. Simulated stalactites on perch provide good grip. Dividers on plasma trough discourage fighting. Bats feed in total darkness, undisturbed by the infra-red floodlight, which produces a bright clear picture in the special viewer provided. (Same type of infra-red viewer as used by CIA for nocturnal missions.) Feeder also doubles as a guano accumulator. (Guano, or bat manure, is prized as the richest known fertilizer.) Unit soon pays for itself; list of U.S. markets included. Detachable easy-clean guano tray. Plasma pellets are universal-donor type for all breeds; just dissolve in warm water and serve.

Feeder with Fan and Beeper; 50 Plasma Pellets; Infra-red Flood and Viewer; Hanging Bracket; Guano Scraper and List of Markets: 169.95

Space-Probe Action Set

This 50 piece action playset gives you the real feel of a space probe. Learn how to handle yourself during liftoff. Avoid aborted launches; know just when to say "We have ignition!" Achieve insertion into orbit. Even dock in space (not under age 10). Experiment with the zero-gravity toilet, eat weightless moon rock candy, and drink Agent Orange Ade™ from sucker-bags, just like the real astronauts. After touchdown deploy your mission flag on the surface. Then try your hand at trouble-shooting the landing module—What do you do if a soil-sampler probe-arm fails to extend? Stick with a moonshot. . .or explore the outer planets, capture an asteroid, and go for meteor parts. All the while keep listening for the voice of nocturnal emission control guiding you to a perfect splashdown. 89.95

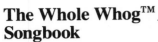

The Whole Whog™ Songbook

A hundred easy-to-play Whole Whog™ favorites. Featuring simplified color-coded notation for organ, banjo, and accordion. Selection includes:

Piggy Sue
Hog on the Range
My Old Kentucky Ham
Swinee River
Hogbreak Hotel
Shanks for the Mammery
Sweet Su-ee
I Want My Piggy Back
Porky and Bess
Sioux City Sow
Days of Swine and Roses
I Wanna Hold Your Ham
Piggyback Rider.   7.99

The Game of Surgery

One false move can kill in this fast-paced and unnerving game of strategy, knowledge and skill. Try your hand at diagnosis and operations on a lifelike computer-patient programmed with every symptom imaginable. Symptoms change in response to treatment. Players compete against the ailment, not against one another; it takes the teamwork of physicians and nurses for the operation to be a success. See if you can land on the right organ with your electronic "scalpel". Slip-ups set off the "complication" alarm—think fast to avoid losing points due to coma or death. If your diagnosis is wrong you lose additional points for unnecessary surgery and malpractice. Live through the drama of open-heart surgery. Can you handle a transplant organ? Pick your way through the brain without touching a nerve. Even give cosmetic surgery a whirl. Enjoy the satisfaction of seeing your patient pull through post-op and resume a normal life. Includes four surgical gowns, masks, and caps.   29.95

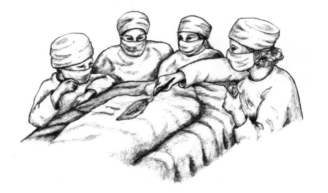

The Third Principle of Pigonometry (The Porcine Principle)

The sine of the porcine is equal to a total effect greater than the wide ankles.

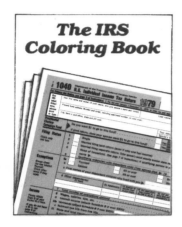

Coloring Books

A departure from the stilted representational style of art in traditional coloring books, these editions have been inspired by Abstract Expressionism, and yet are derived from man-made forms.

The Oil Spill Coloring Book

Contour renderings based on actual aerial photographs of recent major oil spills and offshore well blowouts including Santa Barbara 1969, Marseilles 1978, Tobago 1979, and Gulf of Mexico 1979. The intricate and beautiful patterns of swirls and arabesques with their iridescent rainbow highlights pose a real coloring challenge. No two spills alike. Larger spills are shown in several stages of expansion.   3.95

The IRS Coloring Book

Contains Form 1040, 1040-A, and all the most popular Schedules: Schedules A and B, C, D, E, and SE. Also includes many lesser known forms with interesting grid configurations which are ripe for coloring: Form 5695 "Energy Credits", Form 1310 "Statement of Person Claiming Refund Due to a Deceased Taxpayer", Form 4932 "Laundered Funds", and Form 5807 "Exemptions for the Nonresident Illegal Alien Unmarried Head of Household". Color by number—colors are coded to the actual IRS line numbers.   5.95

The Pizza Coloring Book

Try your hand at a "Sausage Only" and a "Mushroom and Pepper", or for a coloring extravaganza, the "Combination", an elaborate array of ingredients in 20 colors (everything but anchovies). Pizzas are actual size with lifelike details.   4.95

Whole Whog™ Pig Tales

The pig figures big in these tales for young and old alike. Our familiar and engaging barnyard friend, the pig, provides us with much more than meat—he's a source of fun, adventure, information, and sometimes even a little wonder. Choose from our varied library. Hardbound, each: 9.95

Swine and Punishment
A Tale of Two Piggies
Sty Wars
The Prince and the Porker
The Pig and the Pope
Swine Flu Over the Cuckoo's Nest
Pork Noise Complaint
Hamlet (the Francis Bacon version)
Porkahontas
Ivanhog
The Sensual Sow
Pork Futures in a Troubled Commodity Exchange
Slaughterhouse Five
This Little Piggie and the Stock Market
*Stretching Your Jerky—or How to Pig Out While You
    Beat Inflation in the Kitchen*

The Game of Megalomania

Winning is everything in this grueling game of ambition. Blo-Hard™ inflatable pieces (swelled heads) vie for position on the precarious hierarchy of push and shove. "Hands-on" assertiveness training makes for intimidating fun. Push your "one-upsmanship" button to try and advance your position. If your opponent pushes his "collusion" button, you may counter by pushing "betrayal", but *only* if the double-cross is lit up. Push as many buttons as you can; the pushier the better. Remember, you can break the rules, but discovery carries a penalty. See if you can climb to rung number one on the ladder of social standing; then try to hold on to it.   19.95

The Pledge of a Lesion

I pledge a lesion to the lab
Of the united states of medication,
And to the repugnance for which it stands;
One nation,
Under sedation,
With Librium and Valium for all.

Honky Pig™
Jogger's Horn

Whole Whog™ Jogger's Hazard Pack

The question of congestion on our jogging tracks is a serious one. Don't be casual about casualty; be prepared for the menace of jostling joggers with the Whole Whog™ Jogger's Hazard Pack. **The Whole Whog™ Jogger's Airbag Vest** inflates on impact in the event of a collision or fall—just like automotive air bags. Use of the Airbag Vest can make the difference between a bruise and a catastrophic injury. It also provides flotation if you fall into water. **Whole Whog™ Safety Flares** are always on your belt-pack when you need them. In case of an accident, strike anywhere and place them around the scene to warn oncoming joggers of bodies on the track and prevent a pile-up. Heavy traffic calls for the **Honky Pig™ Jogger's Horn.** Use a short blast to clear the right of way and avert disastrous head-on collisions. No need to shout and break your breathing rhythm. Horn operates by a string that hangs down with a weighted "ham" pull; blow it by pulling hamstring.   149.95

The Game of Truth Tricks

There are many paths to the summit, and they're all full of tricks. You'd better be tricky too if you want to come out on top. The game-board is a long-lasting relief map of the Magic Mountain, surrounded by plenty of rough terrain. Move your piece along and see if you can get by the many obstacles and pitfalls. You won't have to go through it all if you can find the short-cuts. Mere stamina isn't enough—you must learn the tricks to the top. Then and only then can you transcend the concept of winning. Start by spinning the Prayer Wheel of Fortune to find out how far you can go; if you're still not clear, pick a card, do a chart, or flip a coin . . . and you're on your way. Avoid landing on the Tree of the Parrots with its hypnotically swaying branches—they'll try to put you out with a magic word. Watch your step in the Forest of the Bent Ones where all the natives are twisted or upside-down—try to make it through without getting bent out of shape. Don't get stuck in the Hut of the Medicine Man where strange chemistry weaves a spell—take a powder right away. Look out for the Parade of the Leaping Monkey-Monks—don't get trampled in their gyrating rapture. And avoid being taken in by the Tower of the Riddle-Master with its revolving door of tricky language that only leads back into itself—your head will be spinning and you'll never get in to see the master. Any number can play, but few are chosen.   14.95

Ham Hockey

The exciting off the wall game of hockey you play in any empty uncarpeted room. Try to hog the puck while carefully keeping behind the center loin, and see if you can score by poking the puck into your opponent's goal. Get down on your hocks, roll around, and shuttle back and forth on the amazing new all-direction ball-bearing knee skates. Ham Hockey is a flurry of lightning action and one-on-one strategy. The irregular shape of the hard rubber puck-"chop" makes it difficult to predict the bounce.

Puck "Chop", "Chop" Sticks, "Feeding Trough" Goals, Center Loin Marking Tape, 2 pair
Knee Skates: 59.95

H and R Blocks

Don't tax your toddler's intellect. Your child learns the alphabet gradually with this set of colorful blocks with H's and R's only. Speech therapists recognize H and R as the two worst stumbling blocks to pronunciation*. Master them first and keep speech and reading blocks from forming. Phase in more difficult sets later: PTA, NFL, CIA, TGIF, USDA, RSVP, LSMFT, AFLCIO, and finally the entire alphabet. Bright primary colors stimulate toddler creativity. Non-toxic.   9.95

*H because it's aspirated, and R because it's a tricky lateral semi-vowel.

Stuck Pig™ Dart Game

Porker Brothers presents fast paced family fun. Accumulate a freezerful of imaginary meat. The board is a butcher's chart of the cuts of pork, the darts are tiny cleavers. Try to land high on the hog, bring home the bacon, or hit a rib; for the big juicy ham, try to stick it in the butt! Real butcher-block-look polyurethane-foam butcher's-chart board, with 12 stainless-steel-look cleavers, and cleaver caddy.   19.95

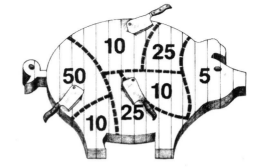

As the pig is bent, so grows the hog.

Houseware
Warehouse

Whole Whog™
Whole Whouse™
Coordinates

You're in the pink with this complete larder of household accessories that features our popular Wistful Piglet™ motif. This collection is gayly colored in the favorite pink pigment of your imagination. A sprinkle of pink'll add charm to every nook and cranny.

Wistful Piglet™
Ceramic Miniatures

Hog Call™ Dinner Bell	2.95
Ham Hocks™ Mail Box	7.95
Pigtail™ Corkscrew	3.95
Pork Butt™ Bookends	7.95
Hogwash™ Laundry Tote	5.95
Hog-Tied™ Macramé Plant Hanger	1.95
Capitalist Piggy™ Bank	1.95
Corn-Fed™ Corn Holders	.95
Big Ham—Little Ham™ Wall Clock	9.95
Wistful Piglet™ Ceramic Miniatures. Complete sty of 12 piglets. Three different poses. Shadowbox with tiny compartments.	8.95
Wistful Piglet™ Toaster Cover Cover. Clear acrylic cover protects your own vinyl toaster cover.	1.95
Wistful Piglet™ Metric Music Box. Lift the lid and piglet sings, "I've gone metric over you..." Metric equivalents are printed on underside of lid.	9.95
Nursing Sow™ Non-Dairy Creamer. Roll her on her side and pour it on.	4.95
Pork Snout™ Coin Caddy. Pays through the nose for the delivery boy's tip.	4.95
Wistful Piglet™ Butcher-Block Chopping Block. With all-around blood gutter.	6.95
Picnic Ham™ Wicker Piggy Picnic Hamper	8.95

Double Knit Picker

Balls? Pills? Synthetic knits are notorious for balling, pilling, and matting. Make them behave this easy new way. Slash a wide swath of smoothness through an unkempt underbrush of neglected balls and pills. Even handle well developed mats; they come clean with just a little stroking. Depiller of strength you can rely on.   4.95

Closet Queen Sachet

Stale corners get fresh with this lovely fragrant
sachet that hangs out in closets. Works in the air and
penetrates clothing too. Comes out of the closet and
sachets around to freshen other areas of the house.
Flaming coral brocade bag and strap. Zippered bag
takes replaceable powder pouches. Patchouli,
lavender, tuna.   39.95

Liquid Hammer™

Fight noise pollution. Hit the nail on the head without a
hammer. This amazing formula drives nails silently
and chemically. Apply one drop on the head and let
stand overnight. The morning after, it's driven home.
No nerve-racking and incessant pounding to drive
your neighbors up the wall. Even wildlife will begin to
return to construction sites. Slow-driving action fights
bending and cracking. Remember: "An ounce of Liquid
Hammer™ is worth a pounding and more."
An ounce: 3.95

Black Hole™ Garbage Disposer

Lost in a space full of waste? Whatever the matter is
in your kitchen, the anti-matter action of the Black
Hole™ can take care of it. Make a mass. Then accelerate those unwanted particles into oblivion. This
compact unit, with its insatiable vortex, neutralizes
waste in no time or space. Put advanced astrophysics to
work in the kitchen sink. No mere quark of design, the
principle of the Black Hole™ is the ultimate in natural
phenomena. Infinite capacity, no external power
source, no plumbing, no discharge, no waiting...and
no matter!   1599.95

Night Life Night Light

Far from being just a dim bulb by the wall, this night
light captures the fun and excitement of inner city night
life by flashing "disco . . . bar . . . casino . . . motel"
in real red neon. Four-message cycle repeats every 30
seconds. Great for insomniacs too—hypnotic effect
of flashing neon really knocks you out. Energy
efficient.   4.95

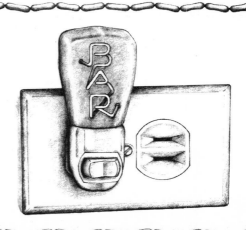

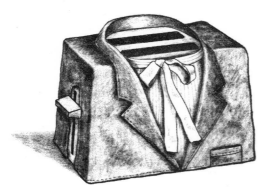

Classic Blazer

Designer Toaster Wardrobe

Every woman loves to dress up her toaster, and now she can do it in style. Now she doesn't have to confine herself to that old traditional vinyl toaster housecoat. She can step out into an expanding universe of sensational designer fashion with this exciting collection of toaster creations.

The Vested Shirtdress

You'll be the toast of the town when your toaster pops up in this poplin concoction that's captivating yet casual. A bright and breezy swirl of unabashed color is deftly paired with a contrasting broadcloth vest and belted with a glistening sliver of silver chain. The effect is expressive of a lithe and lighthearted nonchalance, yet belies more than a glimmer of caprice, even impetuosity. The Shirtdress is in butter yellow, plum preserve, burnt toast, whole wheat, albumin, or lymph. The Vest is in cream cheese or denture ivory. The ensemble: 119.95

The Classic Blazer

A toast to good taste: never overdone, The Classic Blazer achieves eloquence by understatement. Enter: the timeless authority of navy blue cashmere. Your toaster is polished and refined, yet not without a certain unmistakable élan. Whether at luncheon or on the go, the impeccably urbane tailoring and purity of line bespeak a consummate artistry of design that is the hallmark of sophistication. With vented cuffs, French seaming, and flapped patch pockets. Top off your toaster with the moiré Scarf in shimmering triacetate gathered into a blossoming rosette at the slot. Blazer in classic navy only. Scarf in bottle green, terra taupe, town taupe, teal, lapis, amethyst, winter white, lichen, henna, chablis, cola, fudge, oxblood, and pond scum. The ensemble: 289.95

The Evening Gown

The ultimate in toaster wear. A gossamer wisp that's nothing short of devastating. This smoldering heady pouring of intoxication evokes an elusive reverie of intrigue and impalpable fascination. Starting from the scene-stealing bodice, a tumbling cascade of sensuous anti-cling Ephemera III™ in uninhibited indigo dips disarmingly to meet a high empire waist. It then spills over and plunges downward in a long fluidly sculptured column of fluted convolutions—coming to rest at last in a hem stroked with tranquil black sable. The Gown is dramatically framed by a breathtaking Jacket with billowing Kabuki sleeves flounced in a frivolous

splurge of lace. Jacket breasts are embellished with
slender crescents of rattlesnake set ablaze by the
electricity of a myriad of tiny inset opals. Poised on
the shoulder is a beguiling mandala of parrot feathers.
The ensemble: 1789.95

Escape Goat™ Smoke Alarm

This sensitive heat and smoke detector features unusual
kid motif. A loud and heartrending repeating bleat
warns of fire. Big brown eyes light the way to safety.
Tug left horn to test battery; tug right horn to test horn.
Wall-mounted with simulated walnut plaque for easy
within-reach testing and big-game look.   14.95

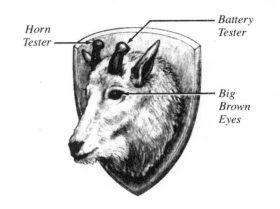

Horn Tester

Battery Tester

Big Brown Eyes

Mister Moss™ Moss Mister

Nothing adds realism to simulated brick like simulated
moss. This handy non-aerosol mister is the easy way
to spray on the luxurious velvety look and feel of real
moss just where you want it. Only your botanist knows
for sure. Permanent, non-sticky, and non-dusting—use
anywhere, even on real brick. Use your imagination.
Dries in seconds, ready to enjoy. Seven ounce
mister: 3.95

Magnetic Maggots

These whimsical refrigerator magnets have the look
and feel of real maggots—the wormlike legless larvae
of certain insects often found on decomposing animal
matter. They'll turn your frig into a conversation piece
and a bulletin board. Soft molded plastic for realism
and no-scratch posting. Tenacious magnets hold tight
and won't pop off—even if you slam the door. Set of 12
maggots: 4.89

Ham
Bacon
Lard
Porkchops

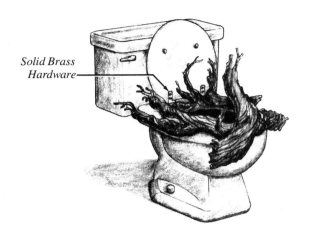

*Solid Brass
Hardware*

Driftwood Toilet Seat

Put an end to hum-drum toilets with the classic appeal of natural materials. These distinctive, sculptural, decorator-look seats are of *real* driftwood, finished in glossy acrylic resin for easy cleaning and long wear. Nature often takes its course without symmetry. No two seats are alike—carefully hand-picked for comfortable and orthopedic contours. Solid brass hardware for the look of solid brass hardware. Fits all standard bowls. Round out the picture with our matching real driftwood bathroom Accessory Ensemble: towel bar, paper holder, tumbler and toothbrush bracket, soap dish, switch plate, robe hook, and bowl brush with caddy. The bottom line on natural comfort.

Seat Only: 39.95
Seat with Accessory Ensemble: 69.95

Sit 'n' Ride Carpet Mower

This is your last-ditch try to save that shag or deep pile carpet when shampooing and steam-cleaning are no longer effective. Without pushing or shoving you're riding high in comfort on a fun-fur seat with plenty of power to pile through. Depth of cut is adjustable for a mere trim or a major harvest. With front discharge, sweeper, and clippings bag. Key-lock ignition prevents unauthorized use.   899.95

The Pick-Pocket™ Pocket Linter

Never again suffer embarrassment in a cash transaction when a load of lint comes up with a handful of change. The Pick Pocket™ provides positively proven pocket protection. Amazing "lint magnet" pad lints your pockets silently as you carry it. Grabs lint and holds it tight, yet will not stick to fingers or currency. Does four pockets in one day, or six small pockets. Great for purses and cuffs too. Even does navels: cut a small piece, insert, leave overnight. (Warning: Do not leave material in navel over ten days. If rash develops discontinue use immediately.) Ten pads: 1.95

Harvest Gold Brightener

Keep America's favorite color bright and pure. Harvest Gold is number one because it's the perfect all-around color: it's not too dark and it's not too light; it's not loud yet it's not muted; it's a natural, liveable, and safe earth-tone without a tinge of hard-to-take primary hues. However, as it ages, Harvest Gold has a tendency to darken to a murky ochre shade; in the presence of prolonged direct sunlight, it may fade to a bland oatmeal tone. This unique formula quickly restores the original vitality of Harvest Gold. Use on blenders, dish drainers, vacuums, refrigerators, ranges, anything in Harvest Gold. (Warning: Do not use on Avocado, Coffee, Almond, or any color except Harvest Gold.) Ten ounce pump-spray   2.95

Microwave Door Knob Warmer

There's nothing as unfriendly as an icy knob. Don't be a snob. Put a warm welcome on your front door for guests who come in from the cold. Rechargeable miniature low-emission microwave generator fits inside all hollow knobs without special installation. Simply charge once and slip it in to keep knob toasty all winter.   7.95

Antler Antenna

Give your set that wild endangered look. Get the luxury and prestige of genuine antler in a high sensitivity indoor TV antenna that pulls in weak stations sharp and clear. Choose from Moose, Caribou, Kudu, and Unicorn. (Unicorn not recommended for metropolitan areas.) Weighted woodgrain swivel base. Guaranteed taken from animals killed only by acts of nature such as forest fire, flood, lightning, disease, old age, auto accidents, meteorites, falling satellites, and non-human predators.   189.95

Caribou

The
Pet
Kingdom

Pool Piranhas

At last a simple natural solution to the problem of pool debris control. Wake up from the nightmare of expensive high-technology systems and their elaborate maintenance. Now you can forget about algae accumulation, filters, pumps, debris traps, chlorination dispensers, vacuuming, skimming, pH testing, sodium bisulphate, soda ash, and diatomaceous earth. Leave it to these amazing fish to digest algae, leaves, dirt, insects, or any solid material in the water quickly, naturally, and without chemicals or exotic hardware. And they discourage trespassers! An isolation net is provided to control fish when pool is in use. Freeze-dried eggs are guaranteed for 20% hatching and 10% maturation; no special incubation needed—just drop in pool. Maintain your own stable population. During seasons when natural scavenging is sparse, prevent attrition by simply sprinkling the pool with our Beads o' Beef™ diet supplement. (Gentle time-release action prevents feeding-frenzies.) In high-debris situations when population gets out of hand, add our Population Control Pellets. Fish will not attack polyethylene net-floats, or vinyl walls of above-ground pools. With set of signs: "Beware of Fish" for front door or gate, and a floating sign for pool, "Carnivorous Fish Beyond This Point". Fish are not recommended for use where there are unsupervised youngsters or aquatic pets, unless a pool cover is used in conjunction with fish. (If pool cover is used, be sure to provide breathing grommets.) Includes instructions for future generations.

Eggs for stocking 15x30 pool, Isolation Net,
Population Control Kit, Set of Signs,
12 Breathing Grommets: 59.95

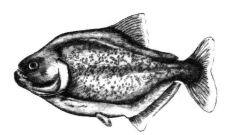

Actual size

Bitch's Britches™ Doggie Heat Shield

A direct application of space program technology, this pair of puncture-proof pyroceramic pants for a bitch in heat acts as an effective and hygienic chastity belt. Do your part to curb promiscuous pet proliferation that flies in the face of urban crackdowns. State waist, inseam, and tail-hole size.   16.95

Live Gerbil Paperweight

An unusual gift item, this functional and personable rodent is so lazy he makes a natural paperweight. These specimens are trained to stay indefinitely without supervision. Complete with intravenous unit for automatic feeding, and cartridge diapers for easy "hands-off" maintenance. Bred for longevity—you can expect a full lifetime of service. Special diet encourages sloth—specimen will not create a disturbance by shuffling around. For active unruly desks that pose a large organizational problem, use *several* gerbils to sit on your piles and keep things running smoothly. (When multiple gerbils are used, specimens will stay put and will not be tempted to visit, but may occasionally call out to one another.) With purchase of three or more animals you get a free kerchief of a different color for each, to color-code your desk-top filing system. Non-shedding.

Single Gerbil with I.V. Feeder, 12 Diapers: 19.95
Three or more Gerbils as above, each: 16.95

Pet Crypt Coffee Table

"The demise of a furry friend cries out no less for a noble memorial."
         —John Milton

Sooner or later in the life of our pet, we must come to grips with the inevitable reality of death. Every creature must meet this moment, each in its own way. As long as there have been civilizations man has felt the need to commemorate the passing of a loved one. Now this simple and practical memorial fulfills that need without a costly burial plot to burden the environment and without the indignities of conventional disposal. Now you can find comfort and satisfaction in the knowledge that the remains of your pet are at rest in an appropriate repository. This elegant monolithic Coffee Table Crypt with clean classic lines to complement any decor is handcrafted in finest granite. With matching ash tray (in case you choose cremation). Engraved custom epitaph is included (up to eight words), or choose one of our standard epitaphs: "Dog Gone", "Cat Below", "Bye Bye Birdie", or "God Loves Your Pet's Name Here".   1295.95

Hog today, ham tomorrow.

Catapult™

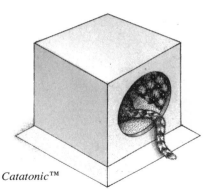

Catatonic™

Think Tank™

Cat Litter Environments

Your cat is a complex creature with needs and idiosyncrasies that are very personal. He can't make do with any old box of sand—it'll cramp his style. For complete self-expression, we offer here an impressive line of Litter Units that are total miniature environments to really put your puss at ease. Each ensemble includes ten pounds of absorbent deodorant litter.

Catapult™

For the high-achiever who's got nothing to hide, this unit is a mini athletic stadium complete with lights, bleachers, scoreboard, crowd noise, and distance markers. Let your little performer put the shot, and see if he measures up. 23.95

Catatonic™

A padded-cell enclosure for the one who wants to work it out in private. With wide tip-proof base for the unstable personality. A real comfort to the cat who can't handle it when things don't come out as planned. This might just be his big breakthrough. 27.95

Think Tank™

A sticky problem is child's play for the cerebral cat. He'll just think it through and get results in a snap. Snugly ensconced in his little stainless steel geodesic dome, he'll have one brainstorm after another. 29.95

Zen Garden™

An exotic setting that's conducive to mind-over-matter.
Zen monastery rock-garden scene has suavely curving
patterns raked in the sand. Bonsai. Your pet adroitly
puts his own contemplation-rocks in place to finish the
picture. Sands are herbal-scented and pH balanced.
Litmus tester and mini rake included.   34.95

Passover™

A kosher unit for the cat who tries harder to advance
the peace process. Shady dwarf-palm oasis and ancient
ruins are surrounded by real Sinai sands for trackless
waste. It's a lazy scene, but this cat knows better than
to just sit there like the Sphinx—he's out for a
payoff.   99.95 or make offer.

Log Jam™

Something for the rugged natural pet that likes to get it
out in the open. A fragrant and inviting mini redwood
forest with log-choked stream and recyclable real
bark-chip litter. This cat finds getting back to nature
a simple matter of elimination.   19.95

Red Herring™

The sly, urbane cat loves intrigue and adventure. Watch
him match wits with this complicated labyrinth of
passageways. Will he come through under pressure?
Sniffing out clues and following traces, he'll feel his
way with uncanny instinct, finally coming out the
other end.   24.95

Zen Garden™

Red Herring™

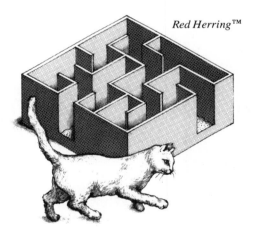

Dogmatic™ Pet Solid Waste Retrieval and Disposal System

A triumph of technology—the ABM (ICBM-interceptor) of pet scoopers. Based on the latest space systems telemetry, this unit is actually a miniature anti-missile missile which knocks out its target in mid-air, before it can reach ground zero. A self-powered mobile launcher tracks your dog, keeping within range yet allowing for pet privacy. When the pavement-proximity sensor indicates that pet's payload is en route, a heat-seeking missile is launched to intercept, enclose, wrap, and hermetically seal the target missile, and parachute it to a soft landing...all in a moment. No more fouling of walkways, no more telltale smear from conventional post-landing manual retrievers. The Dogmatic™ has 3.4 microsecond response time at a maximum range of 14 meters to keep pace with pet waste.

Pet in Launch Position

Mobile Launcher with Heat-seeking Missile

The Minuteman™, for large dogs:	995.95
The Half-minuteman™, for small dogs:	2795.95
The Pee-Wee™, for puppies:	2995.95

Aquarium Eyeglasses

Bring the mysterious spectacles of the undersea world up to the surface to enjoy. These amazing eyeglasses, which are a fully equipped miniature aquarium, provide you with a portable and economical way to have a close-up view of the feeding and breeding cycles of tropical fish. Follow the cavorting of playful guppies, delight in the brilliant light-show of darting neons, and thrill to the graceful ballet of miniature angel fish. Includes instructions for eye exercises to develop short-distance focusing ability. You can watch for hours without strain, and easily alternate between the fish and normal view beyond. Pump, heater, light, and filter are concealed in earpieces. Pump can produce a bubble-screen for privacy—enjoy the fish without being seen by others. Tinted and prescription lenses available. Great for medical and dental waiting rooms. Batteries and fish not included.   29.95

Butcher's Axiom (Corollary to Cleaver's Law)

A chain reaction is only as strong as its missing links and patties—unsolved casings in which minute bits of bacon mysteriously vanish into entropy.

The Prince and the Porker: A Fable

Once upon a time in the faraway land of Lard there lived a portly prince. The people of the prince's province put the prince on a pedestal. The prince was proud of his province and his people, and the people were pretty proud of their portly prince. Yet the poor prince was perturbed. Not because of his portliness, but because he was a prisoner of his priceless possessions and was never free to wallow at will. Once when wending his way wistfully in the woods, the worried and woeful wuler came upon a lone porker pouting in his wallow. The prince exclaimed, "What a fine life you lead, my good porker, lolling in your wonderful wet wallow. Would that I could wallow as you." The pouting porker retorted, "Oh Prince, and would that I could wear your tasty trimmings and wield the power of Your Lardship." The prince paused to ponder. "So be it!", proclaimed the prince. And so the portly prince and the pouting porker changed places. The prince had a badly needed wallow and the porker sat on his throne. The people took the porker for their portly prince and put him on a pedestal. But as time went by, the real portly prince pined for his finery, and the porker longed for his wet wallow in the woods. One night the petulant porker stole away to the woods, and importuned the portly prince, "If it please Your Portliness," he pleaded pitifully, "would that it were as it was!" "It is!" cried the exultant ex-prince, now proudly restored to power. And so prince and porker each took his place in his previous personality and position. The portly prince perked up, and the porker put off pouting.

Moral: He who would wallow well in the world wallows in his own way.

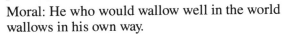

Yard 'n' Garden

Spit not shown

Mercedes Outdoor Grill

No run of the mill grill, this backyard barbecue is the prestige way to enjoy the smokey flavor of charcoal cooking while you spread the smell of success. Advanced design, tasteful appointments, and fine craftsmanship make this unit an investment, not just a grill. Rollabout cart boasts walnut burl handles, power steering, power brakes, push-button dampers, real wire wheels, and radial tires. Includes supple topgrain leather grill cover and five speed diesel spit to handle big birds. Ebony, Ivory, Cognac, Garnet, Anthracite, Platinum.   23,995.95

Automated Lawn Flag System

Dread national holidays? Shrink from the thought of finding and properly displaying Old Glory? Ever want to just forget the whole thing, even at the risk of being thought cynical or unamerican? Then it's time you considered the "flag with a brain"—a full-function flag system for your lawn. Once unit is programmed, pole and flag will automatically deploy on the morning of holidays or any other designated dates. First a concealed grass-covered hatch door in your lawn hinges back; then a 22 foot four-section aluminum pole telescopes up from its underground silo; finally pole rotates to unfurl flag. On low-wind days a rigid rod extends through hem at flag's top edge to spread flag. (Same design as used on first U.S. moon mission flag in thin moon atmosphere.) At dusk flag furls, pole retracts, and hatch closes. Now your flag and pole can be as vandal-proof as your retractable car antenna. Unit has manual override for half-staff occasions. Interchangeable hawk and dove pole-top ornaments. Safety warning bell under hatch sounds when unit is about to deploy. Permanent press flag in full, queen, or king. With book on flag care and display, *Enjoy Your Flag*. Easy installation by contractor.   1395.95

A pig in the pen is worth two in the fen.

Compost Cozy

Help the health of your heap with this insulating cover that works just like a teapot cozy. Bundle up and keep vital heat in to produce the richest compost. Accelerate decomposition of both vegetable refuse and animal waste. Check foul odors and give heap a neat appearance. Non-breathable wipe-clean quilted vinyl shell with polyester fiberfill insulation. In eggshell white, coffee ground brown, and orange peel.　　7.95

Weed Whammer™ Crabgrass Mallet

Come out swinging next Saturday morning and teach that crabgrass a lesson it won't soon forget. Get down on your knees and let loose to stun crabgrass and retard its growth. Break the grip of this unsightly weed and pound it into valuable mulch right on the spot. You can work it out without having to pull it out. Don't worry about whether you've gotten to the root—just beat it into submission. Non-slip grip and one-piece construction so head won't fly off the handle.　　6.95

Pork Barrel™ Hot Tub

Get into getting off together with communal dips. A warm wet wallow works wonders with getting out the kinks. Experience the new sensation of hot mud. The Pork Barrel™ with its built-in Mud Maker™ makes its own mud out of surrounding soil. Gives you perfect consistency every time without tedious stirring, shoveling, and dumping. High speed power pulsator really moves the mud.　　1499.95

Hello Doily™ Disposable Doormat

Lay a doormat that puts out a big friendly hello. Spread a charming lacy doily that conjures up Victorian gentility. A crewel and unusual embroidery whose delicate filigree catches debris from heels. After it's wiped out just replace it. No picking, hooking, and beating. Sixpack:　　8.95

Nonhuman
Pest Control

Sluggo™ Slug Call

Do you shrink from the thought of taking a walk around your own property at night? Don't let mere mollusks make a mockery of your lawn. Put your foot down. Stamp out sickening slugs and their slimy trails of mucus. Crack down on snails too. Use Sluggo™, the top banana of slug calls, to lure slugs from their hiding places for easy mass extermination. Irresistible to all breeds. Works even in dry weather. Lifelike wet-look vinyl. Blow briskly into either end of Sluggo™, and watch a crowd gather.   8.95

Flypaper Wallpaper

Here's an old friend in a new form to help control insects without carcinogens or fluorocarbons. Cut in strips and apply as needed in problem areas. For maximum protection do a whole room. This wallpaper is very tacky—it catches even the largest horsefly, but will not trap small pets. Line cabinets to stop roaches dead in their tracks. Cover picnic tables to blow the whistle on ant traffic. Pre-pasted on both sides for easy application. Washable and long wearing. With removal tongs for large catches, scraper for small catches. Available in a wide range of prints and flocked prints including Strawberry Jam, Honeysuckle, Picnic Scene, Sunbathers, and Carrion. Request free color brochure.

Termite Alarm

Keep from being undermined. We all know that frequent professional termite inspections can be expensive, but not many people are willing to go fumbling around by themselves down in a dark crawl-space for fear of overturning a rock and exposing their pupae. Now this proven alarm system provides an effective and inexpensive way to monitor termite activity continuously. Unit works on the principle of audio discrimination: it can distinguish everyday sounds like voices and telephones from the sound of prolonged muffled chewing. Its high *sensitivity* detects the first crunch of mandible against fir so pests can't get a head start. Its high *discrimination* rules out false alarms. No installation—just set unit on any ground level floor, and like a giant ear to the ground, it starts to listen for trouble. Clever manhole-cover design. (Note: Device has no effect on termites; it sounds the alarm and you take it from there.)   49.95

Rabbit Pelter

Not a skinner. If you're harassed by hares but can't bring yourself to do anything about it for fear of hurting their bunnies, this pelter is for you. At last you can rout rabbits humanely. Pelt pests with a downpour of hard rubber pellets, without penetrating their burrows. Stun without disabling. Based on the design of the famous Catapult of Archimedes. Watch it let fly the next time a pesky hare sets foot in your lettuce patch. 59.95

Death Row™ Bug Pen

Get maximum security against infestation with this pest penitentiary. Once they march through the main gate it's all over—they're under guard until the end. Once and for all, you can punish pests with a capital P. And it's a *humane* penal facility: the ugly job is done with an electric grid—no slow death by starvation. Set an example for bugs on the outside. Even flying ones. Hang it up. Solitary unit serves entire yard, so there's no chance of going over the wall or tunneling out. 34.95

Gopher-Broke™

Beat off the intruder and save far gone lawns with this ultrasonic gopher brainwasher. Unit emits high frequency sound which is inaudible to humans, but which confuses and disorients gophers, and breaks their will to dig. Why put up with the needless despoiling of your property—strike back at these rampaging rodents. Just bury the compact transmitter in your lawn (at least 2 feet deep), and it goes to work immediately, giving gophers the signal to start clearing out. Ten year battery. Will not harm pets on the surface. 39.95

Remember: One *U.S.* hogshead = 63 *U.S.* gallons or 52 *British* gallons, but one *British* hogshead = 63 *British* gallons or 76 *U.S.* gallons.

The Beef Beater™
Ionic Cattle Repeller

Had it with embarrassing unwanted livestock in the home? Had it with the odor, the mess, and the damage? Put the ion effect to work for you, to get rid of cattle without cumbersome traps, dangerous electric prods, or unsightly poisoned cud. This silent positive-ion generator will clear the house within 30 minutes. No more disposal problem and no more danger of stampeding. Unit emits an excess of positive ions, which irritates and repels livestock. Just plug in and watch herds gently scatter. Works even on resistant breeds.   29.95

A Whole Whog™ Pork Tip

Here's a safe and humane way to control flying insects while eating out on the patio: hang up long links of pork sausage to attract the bugs and keep them off you. Everyone gets their share without there being any discomfort or death. Links can be festooned from clotheslines, fences, roof eaves, etc. To add a gala touch hang links with colored streamers and lighted paper lanterns.

Autosuggestion

Road Hog
Hood Ornament

Recapture the romance of the age of the hood ornament. Lovely art-nouveau silverplate sow with her nose in the air and windswept toga calls to mind the carved figureheads on the prows of the great sailing ships of yesterday. Proud pig-headed figure cuts a swath through traffic. Lighted nostrils flash to signal your turn in no uncertain terms. Claim the right of way you deserve.   79.95

Primal Scream™
Human Voice Car Horn

The original form of alarm—and still the most compelling—is the human voice. For safety's sake, put primal scream power in your car. Upgrade your highway language with this five-program horn system for a great range of articulation. Overcome the limited vocabulary of conventional horns. Choose the form of expression that best fits the situation: Punch one button for a gruff baritone repeating "Hey" to make your point with strong emphasis. Punch another for a subtle throat-clearing sound to get results without overdoing it. Select an operatic soprano sustained high note with coarse vibrato, for dramatic musical appeal. And for real trouble, hit the panic button to punch up a child's prolonged scream of terror complete with spasms of raspy gurgles and snorts, and short lapses of voiceless gasping. Or use your own voice—live and amplified—to get across in your own distinctive style. Microphone and five-button selector unit mount directly to steering column; speaker mounts behind grill.   149.95

A Whole Whog™ Haiku

First snowfall on barnyard
covers the sty in lacy white raiment.
Many cloven hooves trample it
into filthy slush.

Meter Beaters™

Beat the meter wherever you go. Slap a high-realism
sticker on the meter window and forget the time. Meter
Beaters™ show time remaining for meter violation. So
take your time and do everything you need to do. The
pointer on the sticker isn't going anywhere.
Field-tested for certified deception (unless under close
scrutiny). Removable adhesive lets you reuse sticker
over and over. You get a variety of stickers to take care
of nearly all municipal meters. Pays for itself after a
few weeks of parking.   7.95

Traffic Ticket Shredder

A discreet way to handle the highly sensitive area of
parking violations. This powerful unit makes short
work of parking citations, non-moving violations, and
even summons up the power for mutilating moving
violations. Also for bills and RSVP invitations. Makes
the narrowest shreds of evidence. Accepts material a
foot wide. Can handle clips. The built-in baler ejects
compacted cubes for deft disposal.   59.95

RV Ivy

Keep your recreational vehicle from looking like a
mausoleum on wheels. Ivy is a natural for an RV. It
gives large RVs a homey appearance, relieving that
stark mobile-home look of large areas of barren siding.
On smaller vans it's an exciting alternative to
airbrushed landscapes. Just clip the planter-boxes and
climbing-trellises to your side panels, plant your
seeds, and in no time you've got a luxuriant wall of
foliage. This strain has been specially developed and
wind-tunnel tested to withstand freeway speeds. And
you never have to water—the patented RV Ivy I.V.™
controlled-flow feeder taps into your RV's water
supply, and automatically does the watering for you.
Negligible wind resistance increases fuel consumption
by less than 1% with normal driving. OK for automatic
car washes.   39.95

Home is where the hog is.

Dashboard Idols

Face it. The dashboard of your automobile is a natural shrine. Your car may be the only place you can find solitude and peace for any length of time. And constant, low-level danger prevents dozing. It's no wonder so many Christians have taken to the contemplation of an icon while driving. Here at last is a selection of figures of great insight or achievement for those of other faiths or secular devotions. Choose from Socrates, Zeus, Pan, Krishna, King Tut, Charlton Heston, Muhammed Ali, Golda Meir, Yassar Arafat, The Ayatollah Khomeini, The Pillsbury Doughboy, The Michelin Man, Tim Leary, Einstein, The Beatles, and Babe Ruth. Porcelain-look non-clammy high-impact polystyrene glows in the dark. Tacky self-stick safety base breaks away if struck in an accident.   2.95

Krishna

The Parking Meteor™

The Parking Meteor™ adapts to any front bumper and turns it into a ram capable of clearing the way for easier parking. Besides opening up tight spots, it will actually create a space where none existed. Pull up to touch the car ahead, brake firmly, and let loose. Enlarge spots up to 50% in a single ram, or double a space in five or six rams. Easy installation.

Parking Meteor™:   89.95
Parking Meteorite™, for subcompacts: 69.95

Whole Whog™ Bumper Strips

Make your point for the people behind you with these fun self-stick bumper strips:

Have You Hogged Your Kid Today?
Have You Kidded Your Hog Today?
Do You Know Where Your Pigs Are?
Honk If You Eat Meat
I'd Rather Be Eating
Butchers Make Better Lovers

White Lettering on ham-red background. Strippable, non-staining.

Single Strip: .95
Whole Whog™ Set of 6 Strips: 3.95

The Hog's Prayer

Our Porker, Wart Hog in heaven,
Wallow be thy name.
Thy pigpen come, thy swill be done,
In the sty as it is in oven.
Give us this day our daily bran,
And forgive us our stains,
As we forgive those who stain us.
And lead us not to mutilation,
Nor deliver us fresh daily.
For swine is the Piglet, the Sow, and the Porker
For ever and ever.
Ah, ham.

Patty Meltdown

This variation on the traditional patty melt is a treat for
the nuclear family. Grill or pan-fry your burger; then
take a slice of process American cheese, form it into a
cylinder and fasten the seam with toothpicks. Pinch the
middle to make a "waist" and flare the open ends
slightly so that it resembles a nuclear plant cooling
tower, place on patty, and return patty to heat. Then
stand back and watch it melt down over patty. Serve
open-faced.

Potpourri

Strident™ Gum

The biggest bubble isn't always the best. Often the top pop is the one that makes the loudest noise. Strident™ is a bubble-gum with a special high-strength membrane that really sounds off when it ruptures. Set a record whether you blow a bubble and explode it or form a flattened cake using the tongue and implode it within the mouth by sucking. Cinnamon, chutney, shark.

49¢

Snort 'n' Squeal™ Snooze-Alarm

This is the first snooze-alarm clock that takes control when you can't, and helps you get back on your feet. The dual alarm system and the built-in snooze-cycle governor keep you from sleeping 'til noon in ten minute stretches. The first thing you hear is a low guttural Snort to rouse you gently. You can reset for the ten minute snooze cycle up to three times, and the gentle Snort will sound after each cycle ends; but if you reset a fourth time, a piercing Squeal takes over to give you the rude awakening you deserve. And you can't shut the Squeal for 90 seconds or reset the Snort cycle for 12 hours. Clever hog's head design: press left ear for Snort reset, press right ear for Squeal-off/Snort-off. Lighted snout. Neat pigtail coil cord.

11.95

Goose Downer

Not a drug. The first goose-down processor for home use. Raise your own gaggle, pluck yourself, and save big. Unit causes no discomfort to your bird. The goose is a renewable resource whose time has come. Down an entire gaggle in an afternoon with this combination plucker, cleaner, and fluffer. Includes free mini library of Instruction Booklets on keeping geese, getting down off the goose, and getting down to work:

Down on the Farm and Downtown
Downer's Guide
Pure Fluff (making comforters)
Hoedown (down and country wear)
Showdown (evening down)
Enjoy Your Gaggle
Fees for Ganders Standing at Stud
Restraining a Plucky Honker (showing the goose
  who's boss)

129.95

The Feature Creature™

Treat yourself to a feast of convenience and meet a feat of product design—The Feature Creature™—featuring features that make rival units seem effete. Portable, rechargeable, and fully automatic. With overload-protected triple-insulated motor. Front-loading filters are disposable, recyclable, and biodegradeable. Submersible self-cleaning grid. Delay-alarm for eccentric loads with remote-programmable delay override. Tamperproof childproof switch grounds for no static shock. Has the no-tip lip with the no-drip tip. Anti-cling all-weather reversible cover is fire-retardant, mildew-resistant, and hypoallergenic. Permanent nonstick coating on front of unit; removable self-stick coating on back (for mounting). Non-toxic non-yellowing shell has the new no-nonsense nonskid base. With self-lubricating joy stick (one hand operation) for control of variable thrust settings. Won't show finger marks. Union made.   589.95

Big Burger Tote

Chuck it all in! Hamburger motif highlights this unusual and practical shoulder bag with big capacity and an impressive array of accessories and cosmetics to keep you beautifully organized. Ensemble includes "process American cheese slice" credit card caddy, "ripple-cut pickle slice" coin purse, "tomato slice" coupon file, "bacon strip" billfold, "onion ring" key ring, "lettuce" hanky, Big Macintosh™ compact-folding raincoat, "ketchup" lip gloss, and "special sauce" liquid blush. There's a hidden compartment in patty, and buns are sprinkled with "sesame seed" sequins. A feast for the eyes. Use with relish on any outing. Add a free personalized touch with a scorched cattle-brand-look monogram.   13.99

Process American Cheese Slice Credit Card Caddy

Bacon Strip Billfold

Ripple-cut Pickle Slice Coin Purse

Onion Ring Key Ring

Tomato Slice Coupon File

Lettuce Hanky

Whole Whog™ Smoke Shop

Pork Longs™

Olympic length that's ready for a marathon.
Millimeters beyond the runner-up. With the towering
tallness that makes for staggering satisfaction.
Carton: 5.95

Swine Slims™

Sleek shape and a taste that comes across without
puffing and panting. Carton: 6.95

Pigarillos™

To the point. Short and severe-looking, yet mild.
At last you can get mildness without sacrificing
a harsh appearance. Carton: 5.95

Virginia Hams™

Clove scented. Regular or pig-mint Menthol. The
most widely smoked ham. Carton: 7.95

Dunghill™

Top of the heap richness. High on the hog, yet low in
tar. Special filter screens out undesirable elements.
Carton: 9.95

Marlwallow™

If you'd rather wallow than fight, this is the mellow
wallow with satisfying full-bodied taste. Pink tipped.
Come to where the slaver is. Carton: 6.95

Surgeon General™ Stop-Smoking Muzzle

If pills, filters, and scare tactics don't do the job, it's
time for something drastic. Crack down and clam up.
Go cold turkey with a muzzle of mesh that provides
positive prevention. Breathe easy with this cancer-
canceling fine mesh smoke screen. Won't slur speech,
and puts an end once and for all to insertion of any
smoking material.   9.95

The Pigthagorean Theorem

For a right angled sty, the slop on any hogpoteneuse is
equal to the sum of the slop on all the other hides.

Bubb-o-Dent™ Gum

We've gone and put the miracle of Teflon in your mouth. Until now denture wearers have been afraid to chew, let alone blow. Well now they can blow with impunity. Bubb-o-Dent is a breakthrough in bubble gum. It doesn't stick to dentures. When bubbles get out of hand and end up on your face it doesn't stick there either. Spearmint, anise, fig. Five slab pack: 39¢

Universal Processor

The first processor with truly universal capabilities. Unit processes everything in every way. Handles all applications, whether residential, commercial, agricultural, or industrial. Reams drains, seals pipe nipples, strips threads and finishes in a flash. Restores old hasps, peens rivets, makes dovetail joints. Will even mill, miter, knurl, and crimp. Spreads manure, gelds calves, and girds loins. Milks and waters too. Bales, battens, bundles, binds, and bonds. Browns and serves. Cores pippins and pits with aplomb. Refreezes thawed peas, refries beans, reconstitutes juice, and reverberates walls. Defrosts, defoliates, deburrs, and delouses (a delouser de luxe). Galvanizes leaders and gutters alike. Debunks solutions, delivers suspensions, decants emulsions, and decocts sediment. Decontrols prices, devalues dollars, and destabilizes economies. Degrades, demeans, defames, deforms, defrauds, and defrocks. Even deviates septums. Includes subscription for a lifetime of attachments as they become available.   1499.95

Universal Detector

Today's world gives cause for alarm. You've got a lot more to worry about than smoke. You need to take heed and get ready for the worst. You need the first detector with truly universal capabilities. It detects the presence of any person, object, substance, emanation, or event—from any source at any distance, through any barrier. Unit beeps in heat, buzzes when it gets wind of escaping gas, cries out for intrusion, and indicates medical emergency or death (attach monitor cell to each family member). Also warns of impending earthquake, airborne pollen, police radar, solar flares, radioactivity on guests, carcinogenic foodstuffs, tax audits, and dirty diapers. Even detects lies. So let the Universal Detector put your mind at rest. The *detector* overreacts—so *you* can relax.   399.95

Weather Potato

Hand-painted ceramic-look potato of rugged PVC material has weather-sensitive "eyes". Smooth eyes mean fair; sprouted eyes mean cloudy with rain likely; sprouted and shrivelled eyes mean storm. Just remember, "Eyes within—sunshine will begin. Eyes start to sprout—don't go out." Now you don't have to guess at the weather—just take it from your tuber.   3.95

Cloudy with Rain Likely

Coffee Table Hatch Cover

A redwood burl coffee table is a natural as a nautical hatch cover. At Whole Whog™ we've created a beautiful match of supply and demand by making available our surplus inventory of burl coffee tables to help fill the shortage of hatch covers in recreational boating and the shipping industry. These are not seconds or repos; they're flawless new coffee tables, and they're drastically marked down so now you can afford to cover those dangerous and unsightly gaping hatches on your boat, whether you need several for a small craft, or dozens for a giant freighter. These coffee tables make attractive and offbeat hatch covers. The irregular shape of the redwood burl relieves the severe symmetry of rectilinear shipboard forms, adding an interesting accent to an otherwise stark deck. Coffee Table Hatch Covers are practical too! Durable deep-gloss plastic resin finish withstands salt water and rough handling by longshoremen. Can even be used as a coffee table by the crew for snacks and card games.

1-9 units:	14.95 ea.
10-24 units:	12.95 ea.
25 or more units:	9.95 ea.

Punchcard Folder/Bender/Spindler/Mutilator

Strike back at faceless authoritarian bureaucracy at home, in the office, or at school. This versatile unit performs one, all, or any combination of the four famous forbidden functions. It disfigures computer punchcards individually or in stacks of ten. With delicate cycle for mini-mutilation: roughs up cards sufficiently to make your point, but does not harm data holes.   19.95

Movies on Hold

Say goodbye to humdrum music tapes on hold. Now you can put people on hold with impunity. They'll be well entertained until you get around to them. Your callers won't mind waiting when they can listen to the original sound track of a great motion picture. Select the sound track that's just right to tailor your telephone tactics to your business:

Gone With the Wind: Insurance Companies
The Towering Inferno: Architects
The Creature from the Black Lagoon: Oil Companies
The Godfather: Family Planning Centers
The Birds: Pet Shops
Jaws: Orthodontists
Cries and Whispers: Hospitals, Rest Homes, and
    Correctional Facilities
Deep Throat: Weight Reducing Salons
Blow Up: Obstetricians
Psycho: Bath Shops
The House of Usher: Theaters
Wait Until Dark: Power Companies
Black Hole: Proctologists
The Wiz: Urologists
Dracula: IRS
Night of the Living Dead: Restaurants
From Here to Eternity: All-purpose engrossing drama
    for the longest wait on hold

Easy hookup—simple tools. Tape unit plus one sound track: 89.95

Pig Pen Desk Set

Wallow in this collection of handsome and hard-working desk accessories. (a) A gold-filled pig pen makes your statement with indelible oink. It rests on a slab of (b) real polished hoof with personalized pigskin nameplate. Set also includes (c) pigtail letter opener, (d) pig's bladder blotter, (e) pig's knuckle cigarette lighter, (f) ash sty, (g) esophagus pencil cup, and (h) pork ribs vertical desk organizer with five rib dividers and expanding spine for increased capacity.   79.95

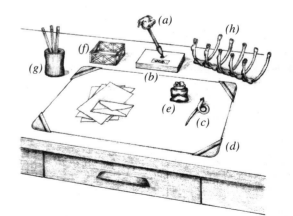

Many hams make light work.

Mother-of-Pearl Handle

Get a grip on the first handle with truly universal capabilities. Amazing suction holds firm to any surface; even defies moisture or grease. A gentle touch and you've got a functional and lovely handle at that place, wherever you want it, ready for manipulation, transport, and admiration. Complement any personal article. Uplift your gift. Things perk up with a good handle of real mother of pearl.   29.95

Lucky Pig's Foot Fetish

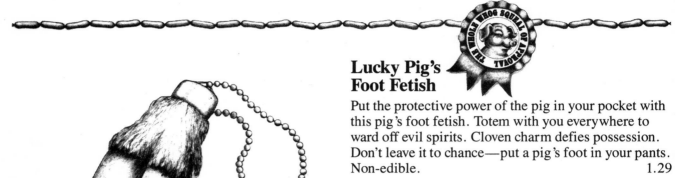

Put the protective power of the pig in your pocket with this pig's foot fetish. Totem with you everywhere to ward off evil spirits. Cloven charm defies possession. Don't leave it to chance—put a pig's foot in your pants. Non-edible.   1.29

Sneeze Saver™

A real gas saver. Save energy and money by harnessing the power of your sneezes, coughs, belches, throat-clearings, etc. Kinetic body energy is a significant natural resource. The average sneeze for example is amazingly powerful, traveling up to 80 feet at speeds exceeding 25 mph; and there are over 3 million sneezes every hour in the U.S. alone. But to date, this great reservoir of renewable energy has gone to waste. Now at last there's a practical way to capture it, store it, and convert it into high-voltage alternating current. This hand-held turbine generator converts the power of a single sneeze into enough electricity to toast three pieces of bread, to operate a garage door opener five times, or to drive a self-propelled vacuum 25 feet. Just place the Sneeze Saver™ firmly over the appropriate orifice at the moment of thrust and hold tight. Thick pneumatic gasket around mouth of unit insures good seal against body so that entire thrust is directed into turbine for maximum yield. When ready-light indicates that charge is sufficient, plug your appliance into the Sneeze Saver™ and you're under power. So don't be polite—let it all out, and let yourself be heard for energy conservation.   59.95

Executive Nut Cups

These traditional festive cups for nuts and candy really perk up Board Meetings. Gathering together to make high level executive decisions need not be a tense or somber occasion. Create a gala atmosphere and help bring Board Members closer for more effective action. Choose from rosewood-look styrene, brushed-chrome-look acrylic, and kidskin-look vinyl. Includes embossed custom monogram of Corporate logo plus Board Member's name in real 14k gold-look acetate. Nuts and candy not included.

Small Business Board set of 8 cups: 39.95
Corporation Board set of 24 cups: 89.95

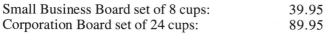

The Faultfinder™ Pocket Calculator

A very calculating companion that has many critical functions and quite a few overcritical ones. It divides assets and multiplies liabilities. In addition, it expresses beratings in four places. Negative logic makes short work of rationalizations. Repeat-key for ongoing multiplication of reprimands. Fixed-idea decimal and automatic fractious overflow. Quick rejection for errors plus highly visible error indicator. Accumulating memory stores objections, then recalls them, and uses them again and again. Self-vindicating. Imputes, impugns, and indicts, then displays it and prints out proof and reproof to back it up. Key for constant castigation and derision, plus negative constant comment. Liquid crystal cheap display takes a dim view. For both science and bookkeeping—take it to task, or call it to account. (Takes no interest, does not discount, no extensions.)   79.95

"Living" Bulletin Board

This fun and functional bulletin board looks like human skin and cries "ouch" when stuck. Lifelike molded flesh-tone polyethylene veneer complete with pores, veins, and hair shafts is bonded to a special half-inch chambered styrofoam. When thumbtack is inserted, styrofoam seems to say "ow" or "ouch". Veneer heals itself so punctures don't show. Clever thumbtacks are lifelike moles, boils, and carbuncles. 18x24 board. Caucasian only. Board, 100
Thumbtacks: 29.95

Classical War Literature Lunch Sacks

Reading while eating is a natural, so don't just chew and stare. Put that time to use. Earn valuable course credit and relive the excitement of the famous military campaigns of classical literature. Pillage, plunder and devastation were the order of the day. Now the six great sacks of antiquity are easy to swallow bit by bit with these six sets of printed lunch sacks. The saga of each sack is printed in sequence on the sacks of each set so there's one entire sack per set of sacks. Large print is easy to read even on a badly crumpled sack. Sacks are of rugged 3 mil polyethylene to stop leaks and odors, yet have the look and feel of recycled biodegradeable sacks. In classic brown kraft.

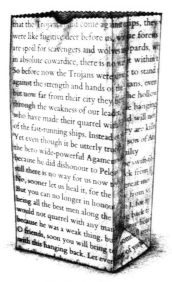

The Sack of Troy

The Sack of Troy	312 sacks	6.95
The Sack of Crete	239 sacks	5.95
The Sack of Carthage	339 sacks	7.95
The Sack of Tyre	291 sacks	5.95
The Sack of Athens	367 sacks	4.95
The Sack of Rome	414 sacks	7.95

Family Member Organizer

Organize your family members with this family message center. Family members get a message whenever they need it. No more dependence on oral communication, and no more hard feelings because they didn't get the message. They get the hard facts, in writing, right in their own slot. When individual family members are satisfied it makes for one big happy family. 3.95

Scratch 'n' Sniff Atlas

Bring home the odors of exotic and familiar lands without leaving your living room. Maps are impregnated with distinctive regional scents. Scratch hard to activate. Jump around. Go on your own olfactory odyssey of ethnic aròmas. Take in a teeming Tokyo fish market. Savor the summer sewage in Venice's Grand Canal. Get a rush hour sniff of a New York subway. Stand shoulder to shoulder under the blazing sun with pungent kibbutz workers in Israel. Catch the bouquet of a cattle-choked Calcutta street. 29.95

Cactus Depilatory

The giant flowering cactus is a fascinating and
fashionable succulent, but you can get a nasty prick.
Make that cactus behave and keep it safe for children
and pets without tedious and dangerous tweezing. This
powerful depilatory solves your thorny problem: just
spray on, let stand for a few minutes, and then hose
down. Spines wash away without a trace. Not
recommended for hair removal on humans.   3.95

San Andreas™
No-Fault Earthquake Insurance
(outside California only)

It's not your fault—so why pay for it? Get comprehensive earthquake coverage with premiums that
won't make you weak in the knees. Protect yourself and your property from the hazards of earthquake and resulting fire, explosion, or tidal wave.
You're also covered in the case of falling objects,
flood and water damage, seepage, leakage, overflow
resulting from or caused directly or indirectly by water
which backs up from sewers or drains or escaping
water from sudden and/or accidental rupture of steam
heating systems due to collapsing, bulging, cracking,
and expansion but not settling of interior or exterior
building walls except as excluded or limited, and the
perils of subsequent riot, civil commotion, vandalism,
pillage, or looting, but not looting committed by the
insured. Request details and sample policy. Then sign
on the crack (if your hand is shaky just make an X) and
rest easy.

Shopper Stopper™
Credit Card Chastity Belt

Clamp down on promiscuous charging by an
indiscriminate family member. Curtail impulsive
shopping that causes later embarrassment and regret.
No need to hide or confiscate card, or lie awake nights
wondering who's charging. Take charge with the
foolproof Shopper Stopper™, an electronic com-
bination-lock of stainless steel that prevents insertion of card into draft imprinter. Soft virgin vinyl
lining won't harm card. Violation of moderation calls
for a crack down. Abstinence makes the heart grow
fonder. Self-control deserves credit—
otherwise forget it.   12.95

Index

About the Authors

Found in the woods and raised by wild peccaries, **Victor Langer** spent his early years rooting for grubs and stealing corn. Under the civilizing influence of progressive toilet training and a Public School education, his development came to hold water. He attended Bard College, where he collaborated with Chevy Chase in creating friction in class; but somber at bottom, he became a touted Teutophile and three-time winner of the Classical Greek Verb Conjugation Bee. He has composed upwards of twelve thousand hypothetical cat-litter brand names, and is an avid proponent of equal rights for garden pests. A reformed sperm bank teller, he currently resides with a budgie incommunicado.

Leslie Anderson has had a checkered career of fine arts, graphic design, snappy patter, and drunk driving. After an idyllic period of seclusion and painting in the south of France, she returned to the academic world to study fine arts and French literature at the University of California at Berkeley. Upon graduation she entered the real world and began her post-impressionable period of painting houses. Her prehensile feet enable her to paint, chew gum, and walk at the same time. She dreams of opening a store for big and tall men. Her mantra is "Oh baby Oh baby." She presently occupies two flats in a San Francisco Victorian mansion with an Irish setter, three gerbils, a snapping turtle, thirty koi fish, four turkey vultures, and a sorrel mare. A professional thumbwrestler, she holds the world cup.

Bob Ross is a noted San Francisco graphic designer and smartass. First suspended from high school by his ninth grade general science teacher for "total lack of humility", he nevertheless graduated with a clear complexion and went on to earn a degree in Philosophy from a California State College. But never able to tell his Hegel from his Schlegel, he gave it up for a successful career of a graphic nature. Although having risen to the position of president in a major design firm, he remains known to all as "Bob Ross". 33 years of age at time of publication, he boasts about 2.2 children, a wife, and the ability to move his eyebrows independently. He is considered by his coauthors to be the least funny of the three.

Acknowledgments

Many shanks to those who lent a helping ham:

Bones Sandy Buddy
Wally Eddy and Chevy